College Reading Skills

Topics for the Restless, Book Four
Stimulating Selections for Indifferent Readers

Second Edition

Edward Spargo, Editor

Books in the Series:
Book One   Book Three
Book Two   Book Four

JAMESTOWN PUBLISHERS

a division of NTC/Contemporary Publishing Company
Lincolnwood, Illinois USA

Topics for the Restless, Book Four

Second Edition

ISBN: 0-89061-530-6

Published by Jamestown Publishers,
a division of NTC/Contemporary Publishing Company,
4255 West Touhy Avenue,
Lincolnwood (Chicago), Illinois 60646-1975 U.S.A.
© 1989 by NTC/Contemporary Publishing Company

Manufactured in the United States of America.
Cover and text design by Deborah Hulsey Christie

8 9 0 VP 11 10 9 8 7 6

Cover credit: Collection: State Museum, Kröller-Müller,
Otterlo, the Netherlands.

Inside Front Cover: AP/WIDE WORLD PHOTOS
2   Sickle-Cell Anemia: Bob Daemmrich/The Image Works
3   The Selling of the Flesh: Ed Birch/UNICORN STOCK PHOTOS
4   Are You Really Ready for the Highways?: U.S. Department of Transportation
5   The Duck Man of Venice: Photograph by Jim Kahnweiler
6   The Right to Exist: Department of the Interior—U.S. Fish and Wildlife Service
7   Dr. Batman: SuperStock International
8   New Use for Old Cars: Jeff Fott/TOM STACK & ASSOCIATES
9   The Anatomy of Drink, I: Copyright Norman Prince
10 The Anatomy of Drink, II: COMSTOCK INC./Tom Grill
11 Textbooks and the Invisible Woman: SuperStock International
12 Atlantis: The Legend Lives On: Greek National Tourist Organization
13 Police Brutality: Answers to Key Questions: Charles Gatewood/The Image Works
14 The Interlopers: Woodcut by Mari SanGiovanni
15 The Plight of the Porpoise: ©New York Zoological Society
16 Organic Gardening in Perspective: USDA Photo
17 Mononucleosis: The Overtreated Disease: Jamestown Publishers
18 Dying, One Day at a Time, I: ©Roger Manley/Southern Light
19 Dying, One Day at a Time, II: Alan Carey/The Image Works
20 Natural Steam for Power: U.S. Department of the Interior/National Park Service

Readability			
Book One	F–G	Book Three	J–K
Book Two	H–I	Book Four	L–up

Acknowledgments

Acknowledgment is gratefully made to the following publishers, authors, and agents for permission to reprint these selections.

Sickle-Cell Anemia by Bern Gentry. Reprinted from *Future* magazine, the official publication of the United States Jaycees.

The Selling of the Flesh by Rog Halegood. Reprinted from *Future* magazine, the official publication of the United States Jaycees.

Are You Really Ready for the Highways? by Norman Richards. Reprinted from *Marathon World,* published by the Marathon Oil Company.

The Duck Man of Venice by Skip Ferderber. Reprinted with the permission of the author and of the *National Humane Review.* Copyright © 1972 by the American Humane Association.

Dr. Batman by Anthony Wolff. Reprinted from *Saturday Review/World,* February 1974, by permission of the author.

New Use for Old Cars by Anthony Wolff. Reprinted with permission of the author.

The Anatomy of Drink, I, II by Rog Halegood. Reprinted from *Future* magazine, the official publication of the United States Jaycees.

Textbooks and the Invisible Woman by Janice Law Trecker. Reprinted from the Council on Interracial Books for Children, Inc.'s Bulletin, with the permission of the author.

Atlantis: Legend Lives On by Arturo Gonzalez. Reprinted from *Aramco World* magazine, a publication of the Arabian American Oil Company.

Police Brutality: Answers to Key Questions by Albert J. Reiss, Jr. Published by permission of Transaction, Inc., from *Transaction,* Vol. 5, No. 5. Copyright © 1968 by Transaction, Inc.

The Interlopers. From *The Complete Short Stories of Saki* by H. H. Munro. All rights reserved. Reprinted by permission of the Viking Press, Inc.

Contents

1 | Introductory Selection

Explains How the Text is Organized and
How to Use It to Maximum Advantage

Vocabulary—The five words below are from the story you are about to read. Study the words and their meanings. Then complete the ten sentences that follow, using one of the five words to fill in the blank in each sentence. Mark your answer by writing the letter of the word on the line before the sentence. Check your answers in the Answer Key on page 106.

A. intent: purpose

B. distribution: arrangement; organization

C. consecutively: in order; one after another

D. corresponding: matching

E. efficient: performing a task easily and skillfully

_____ 1. A wide _____ of topics is needed in order to appeal to all readers.

_____ 2. If you read each chapter _____, you will understand the lessons more easily.

_____ 3. As you work through each selection, you will become more _____ at analyzing written material.

_____ 4. After finishing the book, you will have a good grasp of its _____ .

_____ 5. The skilled reader has learned that each kind of reading matter demands a _____ reading technique.

_____ 6. The exercises cover a wide _____ of reading and study skills.

_____ 7. In order to be an _____ reader, you must sharpen your critical reading skills.

_____ 8. To communicate with their readers is the _____ of all authors.

_____ 9. Answer the vocabulary questions by writing the letter _____ to the correct word.

_____ 10. Answer the questions _____, and then turn to the answer key to correct your work.

(Before you begin reading this selection, turn to page 8 and record the hours and minutes in the box labeled *Starting Time* at the bottom of the second column. If you are using this text in class and your instructor has made provisions for timing, you need not stop now; read on.)

You are using this text for two purposes: (1) to improve your reading skills, and (2) to read articles and selections designed to make you think. Not every selection will be so demanding, however; many articles were chosen just for pure reading pleasure and enjoyment.

These selections span the range of human experience. It was the intent of the editor to find and include writings which show the real world, the world we all have to face daily. On these pages you will read and learn about current problems facing our society: the use of alcohol and other drugs, the struggle of women for recognition and independence, the seemingly unsolvable problem of disposing of garbage and other wastes of industrial production.

Many selections deal with the quality of our environment and possible new life-styles we may be forced to adopt in the future unless we deal now with air and water pollution, population growth, supplying food needs, caring for the homeless and aged with dignity and respect.

However, many selections treat some of the more pleasant concerns of today's older and more mature student. And finally, some selections just make for enjoyable reading.

Do not expect every selection to be equally interesting to you. In such a wide distribution of subject matter there are bound to be stories which will turn you on, but turn others off. Selections which may bore you, and therefore be hard to read and understand, may very well spark the interest of another reader.

A serious student, therefore, will approach each selection in this text with equal enthusiasm and a determination to succeed. This is the kind of attitude to develop toward reading—an attitude which will serve you well for the rest of your life.

The other purpose for using this text, that of reading and study improvement, recognizes reality, too: the reality of today. This text will help you to develop skills and techniques necessary for efficiency in our society.

Included in each selection are two Study Skills exercises. In these, you will learn methods of understanding, critical thinking skills, techniques of comprehension, and many other key ways to improve your reading ability. Both Study Skills exercises are designed to assist you in developing efficient reading techniques. As you read the selections in this book, you will find that often one Study Skills exercise leads directly to the next. It is important to read

It was the intent of the editor to find and include writings which show the real world, the world we all have to face daily.

and work the Study Skills exercises consecutively in order to understand fully each subject.

Today's reader must be flexible enough to choose from a supply of skills one that is suitable for each reading task. The skilled reader has learned that each kind of reading matter demands a corresponding reading technique—there is no single "best" way to read. As you complete the selections and exercises in this book, you will find yourself growing in technique.

Using the Text

The twenty selections are designed to be read in numerical order, starting with the Introductory Selection and ending with Selection 20. Because the selections increase in difficulty as you progress through the book, the earlier ones prepare you to handle successfully the upcoming ones.

Here are the procedures to follow for reading each selection.

1. Answer the Vocabulary Questions. Immediately preceding each selection is a vocabulary previewing exercise. The exercise includes five vocabulary words from the selection, their meanings, and ten fill-in-the-blank sentences. To complete each sentence you will fill in the blank with one of the five vocabulary words.

Previewing the vocabulary in such a fashion will give you a head start on understanding the words when you encounter them in the selection. The fill-in-the-blank sentences present each word in context (surrounding words). That provides you with the chance to improve your ability to use context as an aid in understanding words. The efficient use of context is a valuable vocabulary tool.

After you have filled in the blanks in all ten sentences, check your answers in the Answer Key that starts on page 106. Be sure you understand the correct meaning of any wrong answers.

2. Preview before Reading. Previewing acquaints you with the overall content and structure of the selection before you actually read. It is like consulting a road map before taking a trip: planning the route gives you more confidence as you proceed and, perhaps, helps you avoid any unnecessary delays. Previewing should take about a minute or two and is done in this way:

a) Read the Title. Learn the writer's subject and, possibly, his point of view on it.

b) Read the Opening and Closing Paragraphs. These contain the introductory and concluding remarks. Important information is frequently presented in these key paragraphs.

c) Skim through. Try to discover the author's approach

to his subject. Does he use many examples? Is his purpose to sell you his ideas? What else can you learn now to help you when you read?

3. Read the Selection. Do not try to race through. Read well and carefully enough so that you can answer the comprehension questions that follow.

Keep track of your reading time by noting when you start and finish. A table on page 110 converts your reading time to a words-per-minute rate. Select the time from the table that is closest to your reading time. Record those figures in the boxes at the end of the selection. There is no one ideal reading speed for everything. The efficient reader varies his speed as the selection requires.

Many selections include a brief biography. Do not include this in your reading time. It is there to introduce you to the writer. Many of the selections have been reprinted from full-length books and novels. If you find a particular selection interesting, you may enjoy reading the entire book.

4. Answer the Comprehension Questions. After you have read the selection, find the comprehension questions that follow. These have been included to test your understanding of what you have read. The questions are diagnostic, too. Because the comprehension skill being measured is identified, you can detect your areas of weakness.

Read each question carefully and, without looking back, select one of the four choices given that answers that question most accurately or most completely. Frequently all four choices, or options, given for a question are *correct*, but one is the *best* answer. For this reason the comprehension questions are highly challenging and require you to be highly discriminating. You may, from time to time, disagree with the choice given in the Answer Key. When this happens, you have an opportunity to sharpen your powers of discrimination. Study the question again and seek to discover why the listed answer may be best. When you disagree with the text, you are thinking; when you objectively analyze and recognize your errors, you are learning.

The Answer Key begins on page 106. Find the answers for your selection and correct your comprehension work. When you discover a wrong answer, circle it and check the correct one.

The boxes following each selection contain space for your comprehension and vocabulary scores. Each correct vocabulary item is worth ten points and each correct comprehension answer is worth ten points.

Pages 111 and 112 contain graphs to be used for plotting your scores and tallying your incorrect responses.

On page 111 record your comprehension score at the appropriate intersection of lines, using an *X*. Use a circle, or some other mark, on the same graph to record your vocabulary results. Some students prefer to use different color inks, or pencil and ink, to distinguish between comprehension and vocabulary plottings.

On page 112 darken in the squares to indicate the comprehension questions you have missed. By referring to the Skills Profile as you progress through the text, you and your instructor will be able to tell which questions give you the most trouble. As soon as you detect a specific weakness in comprehension, consult with your instructor to see what supplementary materials he or she can provide or suggest.

A profitable habit for you to acquire is the practice of analyzing the questions you have answered incorrectly. If time permits, return to the selection to find and underline the passages containing the correct answers. This helps you to see what you missed the first time. Some interpretive and generalization type questions are not answered specifically in the text. In these cases bracket that part of the selection that alludes to the correct answer. Your instructor may recommend that you complete this step outside of class as homework.

5. Complete the Study Skills Exercises. Following the comprehension questions in each chapter is a passage on study skills. Some of the sentences in the passage have blanks where words have been omitted. Next to the passage are groups of five words, one group for each blank. Your task is to complete the passage by selecting the correct word for each of the blanks.

Next are five completion questions to be answered after you have reread the study skills passage.

The same answer key you have been using gives the correct responses for these two study skills exercises.

If class time is at a premium, your instructor may prefer that you complete the exercises out of class.

The following selections in this text are structured just like this introductory one. Having completed this selection and its exercises, you will then be prepared to proceed to Selection 2.

Starting Time		Finishing Time	
Reading Time		Reading Rate	
Comprehension		Vocabulary	

Comprehension— Read the following questions and statements. For each one, put an *x* in the box before the option that contains the most complete or accurate answer. Check your answers in the Answer Key on page 106.

1. How much time should you devote to previewing a selection?
   - ☐ a. Your time will vary with each selection.
   - ☐ b. You should devote about one or two minutes to previewing.
   - ☐ c. No specific time is suggested.
   - ☐ d. None—the instructor times the selection.

2. The way that the vocabulary exercises are described suggests that
   - ☐ a. the meaning of a word often depends on how it is used.
   - ☐ b. the final authority for word meaning is the dictionary.
   - ☐ c. words have precise and permanent meanings.
   - ☐ d. certain words are always difficult to understand.

3. The writer of this passage presents the facts in order of
   - ☐ a. importance.   ☐ c. time.
   - ☐ b. purpose.   ☐ d. operation.

4. *Topics for the Restless* is based on which of the following premises?
   - ☐ a. All students are restless.
   - ☐ b. Some students learn best when they are restless.
   - ☐ c. Writings dealing with real problems and situations should interest many students.
   - ☐ d. All of the selections in this text should interest all students.

5. How does the writer feel about reading speed?
   - ☐ a. It is a minimal aspect of the total reading situation.
   - ☐ b. It is second (following comprehension) in the ranking of skills.
   - ☐ c. It is connected to comprehension.
   - ☐ d. It should be developed at an early age.

6. The introductory selection
   - ☐ a. eliminates the need for oral instruction.
   - ☐ b. explains the proper use of the text in detail.
   - ☐ c. permits the student to learn by doing.
   - ☐ d. allows for variety and interest.

7. The introductory selection suggests that
   - ☐ a. most readers are not flexible.
   - ☐ b. students should learn to use different reading skills for different types of reading matter.
   - ☐ c. students today read better than students of the past did.
   - ☐ d. twenty selections is an ideal number for a reading improvement text.

8. The overall tone of this passage is
   - ☐ a. serious.   ☐ c. humorous.
   - ☐ b. suspenseful.   ☐ d. sarcastic.

9. The author of this selection is probably
   - ☐ a. a doctor.   ☐ c. an educator.
   - ☐ b. an accountant. ☐ d. a businessman.

10. The writer of this passage makes his point clear by
   - ☐ a. telling a story.
   - ☐ b. listing historical facts.
   - ☐ c. using metaphors.
   - ☐ d. giving directions.

Comprehension Skills

1. recalling specific facts	*6. making a judgment*
2. retaining concepts	*7. making an inference*
3. organizing facts	*8. recognizing tone*
4. understanding the main idea	*9. understanding characters*
5. drawing a conclusion	*10. appreciation of literary forms*

Study Skills, Part One—Following is a passage with blanks where words have been omitted. Next to the passage are groups of five words, one group for each blank. Complete the passage by selecting the correct word for each of the blanks.

Dictionary Skills

1. Locating Words in Alphabetical Order. One way to speed up word location is to gain proficiency in ___(1)___ words in alphabetical order. Dictionaries, as you know, list words alphabetically, so the faster you can find a word, the sooner you have the information you need.

(1)   writing   locating
        placing   using   recognizing

2. Using Guide Words. To help you find words quickly, dictionaries print guide words at the top of each page. These tell you the first entry and the last entry for that page. Because entries are listed __(2)__ , a glance at the guide words will tell you which words are on that page.

3. Identifying Variant Spellings. Some words can be __(3)__ spelled in more than one way. For example, *practice* can also be spelled *practise*. Variant spellings preferred in England, such as *colour*, are labeled *Brit.* Your book might list only the more popular form.

4. Using the Appropriate Meaning. Most common words have several meanings. One dictionary shows forty-four definitions for the word *go*. You must be careful to choose exactly the right meaning that __(4)__ the sense of the material you are reading.

With just a little practice, you will be amazed to find that the simple act of using a dictionary __(5)__ will make your school work easier and will markedly improve your grades.

We will assume that you have a good, hardcover, college-level, desk dictionary as a basic __(6)__ of your trade. Paperback or pocket-sized dictionaries and supermarket giveaways are just not __(7)__ enough to use for studying. However, if you are about to purchase your first dictionary, ask your instructor for a list of those more frequently recommended for school use.

(2)	carefully	alphabetically
	creatively	rapidly	logically

(3)	concisely	correctly
	continually	conventionally	conveniently

(4)	furthers	fits
	enriches	remedies	contradicts

(5)	immediately	lazily
	occasionally	regularly	eagerly

(6)	remembrance	option
	improvement	symbol	tool

(7)	strong	thick
	complete	popular	heavy

Study Skills, Part Two—Read the study skills passage again, paying special attention to the lesson being taught. Then, without looking back at the passage, complete each sentence below by writing in the missing word or words. Check the Answer Key on page 106 for the answers to Study Skills, Part One, and Study Skills, Part Two.

1. Skill in finding words in alphabetical order results in obtaining needed _____ quickly.

2. Guide words indicate the first and last word entries on a _____ .

3. If only one spelling of a word is offered, it may be the more _____ form.

4. It is important to choose the meaning of the word that is _____ for the material you are reading.

5. It is a good idea to obtain the dictionary that is _____ by your school.

2 | Sickle-Cell Anemia

by Bern Gentry

Vocabulary—The five words below are from the story you are about to read. Study the words and their meanings. Then complete the ten sentences that follow, using one of the five words to fill in the blank in each sentence. Mark your answer by writing the letter of the word on the line before the sentence. Check your answers in the Answer Key on page 106.

A. zealous: very eager

B. immunity: protection

C. alleviate: ease; reduce

D. precipitated: brought about; caused

E. viable: able to function; usable

_____ 1. Some people have a natural _____ to malaria.

_____ 2. Medicine can _____ the pain caused by sickle-cell anemia.

_____ 3. Currently there is no _____ cure for sickle-cell anemia.

_____ 4. Army drill instructors have a reputation for _____ execution of their duties.

_____ 5. White Africans do not have the same _____ to certain diseases that many black Africans have.

_____ 6. For someone with sickle-cell anemia, a crisis can be _____ by high altitudes.

_____ 7. Even the most _____ researchers have not found a way to wipe out sickle-cell anemia.

_____ 8. The death of the Fort Bliss soldiers was not _____ by an abusive drill sergeant.

_____ 9. Education is one _____ way to reduce the dangers of sickle-cell anemia.

_____ 10. There is evidence that certain drugs can _____ the suffering of people with sickle-cell anemia.

In 1970 four United States black soldiers died while on maneuvers. Surprising? No, not really, except the soldiers were not in Vietnam, Laos, or Cambodia. They were at Fort Bliss, Texas. Their deaths resulted from ignorance and neglect not from an overzealous drill instructor but from the failure of the general public and the medical community to recognize a major health problem—sickle-cell disease. With knowledge of the disease, of its effects, and with proper counseling, the deaths of those four young men could have been lastingly prevented.

The problem is finding out who has the disease.

Sickle-cell disease is a disease of the blood that can cause grave injury and death. Hemoglobin, the fluid in our blood cells that makes them red, is the substance that takes oxygen from our lungs to the rest of our bodies. With exertion and muscle usage, hemoglobin uses oxygen and in most of us remains a fluid while returning to the lungs for more oxygen. Sickle-cell hemoglobin is fluid when carrying oxygen, but when oxygen is absent the hemoglobin becomes solid, changing the normally doughnut-shaped red blood cells into a sickle, or new-moon, shape. The result is painful, damaging, and sometimes fatal. When the cells sickle they no longer pass freely through smaller blood vessels; thus, a "log jam" occurs within the vessels. This causes pain and destruction of the cells resulting in anemia. In more severe instances it causes tissue loss or even "necrosis"—the loss of an entire organ. Should this "jamming" occur extensively throughout the body, death will result.

Understanding the Disease

Sickle-cell disease is not contagious; it is inherited through the parents. While sickle-cell disease can cause the damage mentioned above, it does not happen to every sufferer of "sickling." The majority of "sicklers" have two sorts of hemoglobin: sickle-cell and normal, with the type depending on the genes inherited from the parents. Half of one's hemoglobin is received from the mother and half from the father. Assuming both parents have normal hemoglobin, their offspring will have hemoglobin type AA. If one parent has "sickling" hemoglobin and the other has normal hemoglobin the child will be a "sickler" typed as AS. This child then has "sickle-cell trait" and is almost always healthy. Sickle-cell trait is *usually* harmless. But not always. It can be harmful, even fatal, if there is a severe reduction of oxygen like that occurring at high altitudes, from a complicating anaesthetic, from severe lung disease, from lengthy obstructed blood flow after unusually strenuous exercise, from the result of extreme exposure to cold, or complications from other serious diseases. The four soldiers at Fort Bliss had sickle-cell trait, not sickle-cell disease. An individual with sickle-cell disease, typed SS, had parents who both had sickle-cell traits: AS + AS = SS. Such an individual will have anemia and attacks of pain and fever. He may be underdeveloped. He may die at a young age. The disease first causes illness between six months and five years of age. Sickle-cell disease is inherited predominantly by blacks. It is believed to have come from Africa where people with sickle-cell hemoglobin had a natural immunity to malaria. Mediterranean anemia which affects Greeks and Italians is similar to sickle-cell, and is likewise a preventive against malaria. Sickle-cell anemia is a genetic problem among blacks just as cystic fibrosis, hemophilia, and leukemia are genetic problems predominant in whites.

While sickle-cell disease is not contagious, it also is not readily preventable or curable, although it is treatable. Only the *symptoms* of sickle-cell disease, or sickle-cell anemia, can be treated. When the cells sickle and blood flow ceases, drugs are used to ease pain and to alleviate dehydration and constriction of the blood vessels. New, more immediate forms of treatment are being researched. At present, the only form of prevention is testing for sickle-cell trait in individuals. It is estimated that there are two million people in the United States with sickle-cell trait. Each individual should know if they have inherited the sickle type of hemoglobin not only to make reasoned decisions in family planning but, also, to avoid conditions that might bring on a crisis precipitated by high altitudes and overexertion.

What Should Be Done

At present, the most effective means of controlling sickle-cell disease are improved communication and education, plus large-scale testing programs. The average person has limited knowledge about sickle-cell disease, its cause, its symptoms, its dangers, and its treatment. Black communities need more in-depth information and counseling as does the general public. Less than half of the black population has ever heard of this disease. The economic, educational, social, and psychological effects of sickle-cell disease affect all of us. Mass education along with massive testing programs can alleviate much of sickle-cell's dangers. As mentioned earlier, awareness that one has the disease prevents problems. Unfortunately, one can live an entire lifetime and be unaware that he or she has sickle-cell trait. For instance, Indiana University tested 275 persons in a six-month span and found that 112 of them needed to return to the university for genetic counseling. A similar test conducted by the same institution at a foundry in Indianapolis revealed 10 out of 113 employees with sickle-cell trait—all were totally unaware of it. The point? Now these people can avoid situations which might bring on a crisis and have other family members tested and counseled.

At present there are special blood tests used to detect sickle-cell disease but only one that is truly thorough. In recent years, a test has been devised and improved upon by Dr. Robert M. Nalbandian, M.D., that requires only a small drop of blood from a finger. Called the Sickledex, it shows sickling if it is present; yet, to establish the specific type of sickle-cell condition, whether full-disease or a trait, a test using blood drawn from the arm, electrophoresis, is a must. Besides being more thorough, electrophoresis has the added advantage of being cheaper than Sickledex and equally efficient for primary screening. The extensive equipment used by Indiana University cost approximately $1,000. To equip a smaller community clinic or mobile lab would cost a fraction of the above. Cost can no longer be cited as too prohibitive to mount an attack on sickle-cell anemia.

The goals of such organizations as the Foundation for Research and Education in Sickle-Cell Disease and the Southeastern Wisconsin Sickle-Cell Center should and can be the viable goals of any community's clubs and concerned organizations. They can conduct community information programs for patients and the public. They can encourage health officials and legislators to provide increased funds for research and health services. They can initiate and develop facilities for testing and counseling.

Tragedies like the one that occurred at Fort Bliss are preventable. Alleviating the problem of sickle-cell disease does not necessarily require money; however, it does require effort, information, time, and genuine concern. And work should begin now.

The blacks in the United States have enough problems; infirmity and death from sickle-cell conditions should not be one of them.

Starting Time		Finishing Time	
Reading Time		Reading Rate	
Comprehension		Vocabulary	

Comprehension— Read the following questions and statements. For each one, put an *x* in the box before the option that contains the most complete or accurate answer. Check your answers in the Answer Key on page 106.

1. Mediterranean anemia is nature's way of protecting Greeks and Italians from
   - ☐ a. sickle-cell anemia.
   - ☐ b. malaria.
   - ☐ c. leukemia.
   - ☐ d. dehydration.

2. The Fort Bliss tragedy could have been avoided if the
   - ☐ a. soldiers had been in Vietnam.
   - ☐ b. military doctors had been alert.
   - ☐ c. military had been less demanding.
   - ☐ d. soldiers had received proper food.

3. People with sickle-cell anemia suffer their first bout with the illness
   - ☐ a. at birth.
   - ☐ b. between six months and five years of age.
   - ☐ c. between the ages of five and ten.
   - ☐ d. as teenagers.

4. The main thrust of the selection is directed at
   - ☐ a. alarming the black population.
   - ☐ b. criticizing the medical profession.
   - ☐ c. disseminating information.
   - ☐ d. resisting change.

5. It can be concluded that
   - ☐ a. certain races are predisposed to certain diseases.
   - ☐ b. persons of African descent are immune to malaria.
   - ☐ c. the Mediterranean part of the world is unhealthy.
   - ☐ d. military doctors lack professional ethics.

6. Communities should act now to
   - ☐ a. discourage people with the sickle-cell trait from having children.
   - ☐ b. screen people for immunity to malaria.
   - ☐ c. set up programs to test people for the sickle-cell trait.
   - ☐ d. change the physical requirements for military service.

7. Military service is
   - ☐ a. not dangerous for individuals with the sickle-cell trait.
   - ☐ b. not an attractive option for blacks.
   - ☐ c. one cause of necrosis.
   - ☐ d. physically demanding.

8. The tone of the selection is
   - ☐ a. snide.
   - ☐ b. bitter.
   - ☐ c. cautionary.
   - ☐ d. whining.

9. Many blacks are
   - ☐ a. unaware of sickle-cell anemia.
   - ☐ b. fearful of those with sickle-cell anemia.
   - ☐ c. disgusted by the public's attitude toward sickle-cell anemia.
   - ☐ d. unsympathetic to those with sickle-cell anemia.

10. The passage ". . . thus, a 'log jam' occurs within the vessel" is an example of
   - ☐ a. a metaphor.
   - ☐ b. a simile.
   - ☐ c. an alliteration.
   - ☐ d. a hyperbole.

Comprehension Skills

1. recalling specific facts	6. making a judgment
2. retaining concepts	7. making an inference
3. organizing facts	8. recognizing tone
4. understanding the main idea	9. understanding characters
5. drawing a conclusion	10. appreciation of literary forms

Study Skills, Part One—Following is a passage with blanks where words have been omitted. Next to the passage are groups of five words, one group for each blank. Complete the passage by selecting the correct word for each of the blanks.

Editing Your Work, I

After writing a theme or essay, the next step is to read and edit it. This is the time to polish your writing, __(1)__ out the rough spots, and correct any errors.

It is a mistake to suppose that a __(2)__ piece of work can result from just one writing. Everyone needs to work from a rough draft, polishing and editing to arrive at a truly finished product. Skilled writers revise several times because they have learned that with each __(3)__ , an improved version is produced. At least one rewrite is essential to make a paper acceptable. When proofing and editing the first copy, follow these steps.

1. Read for Effect. After writing your paper, read it __(4)__ to see if your words create the effect intended. Does it sound the way you want it to?

Certain __(5)__ of agreement and usage will be obvious when heard out loud. Generally, though, listen for impact, and determine if the paper puts across your ideas in the way you __(6)__ .

2. Review Sentence Structure. Be alert for incomplete thoughts (sentence fragments) and run-on sentences or comma splices. Each sentence should express a complete __(7)__ . Excessively long, involved, or unclear sentences confuse the reader. Search for a more concise and accurate way to express your ideas. Look for ways to combine thoughts; connect sentences that are related.

(1)	smooth	cancel
	round	sleek	throw

(2)	required	inferior
	satisfactory	completed	consistent

(3)	suggestion	conclusion
	reading	copying	editing

(4)	carefully	slowly
	silently	aloud	quickly

(5)	rules	corrections
	errors	choices	areas

(6)	indented	inspired
	intended	edited	explained

(7)	result	theory
	presentation	thought	reason

Study Skills, Part Two—Read the study skills passage again, paying special attention to the lesson being taught. Then, without looking back at the passage, complete each sentence below by writing in the missing word or words. Check the Answer Key on page 106 for the answers to Study Skills, Part One, and Study Skills, Part Two.

1. After you finish _____ an essay, it needs to be edited.

2. At least one rewrite is _____ to make a paper acceptable.

3. Read the paper aloud to see if it _____ the way you want it to.

4. Unclear sentences _____ the reader.

5. Look for concise and accurate ways to express your _____ .

3 The Selling of the Flesh

by Rog Halegood

Vocabulary—The five words below are from the story you are about to read. Study the words and their meanings. Then complete the ten sentences that follow, using one of the five words to fill in the blank in each sentence. Mark your answer by writing the letter of the word on the line before the sentence. Check your answers in the Answer Key on page 106.

A. annals: historical records

B. haunt: a place frequently visited

C. winsome: charming

D. callous: emotionally hardened

E. heinous: very wicked; abominable

_____ 1. The traditional image of prostitutes is of _____ women with hearts of gold.

_____ 2. New York's East Village is a favorite _____ of many young hookers.

_____ 3. Pimps devise _____ punishments for hookers who try to cheat them out of money.

_____ 4. Today most prostitutes have a _____ attitude toward their "johns."

_____ 5. The Southwest ghetto of Washington, D.C., is the _____ of prostitutes such as 17-year-old Lorrie X.

_____ 6. Today's prostitutes are not likely to have _____ personalities and glamorous life-styles.

_____ 7. Prostitution is a recurring theme in the _____ of America.

_____ 8. Some girls have suffered _____ tortures at the hands of their pimps.

_____ 9. Doctors who treat prostitutes for VD hear these women make many _____ comments.

_____ 10. The _____ of American history are filled with stories of fun-loving whores and elegant bordellos.

It is impossible to say how many individuals in the United States are selling their bodies in full or part-time employment for the purposes of sex. One estimate is that there are a minimum of 75,000 professional prostitutes at work during any given evening in the land of free enterprise. But it is the amateurs in the trade that are swelling the figure to perhaps ten times that estimate. These are the female and male hustlers who are turning "tricks" on street corners all across the nation with a rising frequency that has outstripped the capabilities of the law enforcement agencies to control the traffic. It is these "amateurs" that are posing the most serious threat of disease and crime ever known in the annals of American prostitution.

Prostitution is growing. Its sadness fills the land.

(wherein Barbra Streisand played a working girl without so much as having to sing a note), and *Klute* with Jane Fonda in a fully exposed role.

It is easy to see why whores exert such a stronghold on literature and art (Rimbaud was their greatest poet; Toulouse-Lautrec and Hogarth their best artists). For one thing, it is such a basic, albeit base profession. It is the one calling open to all women. It is also, in a sense, the epitome of self-made professions. A girl, dealing solely on her wits (some famous prostitutes have been appallingly ugly) can work her way up from a two-buck hooker to a woman splendidly kept in a fashionable penthouse. At least, that's the theory. Today, however, the realities of prostitution—and the chances for advancement—are of a far grimmer nature than those of our past fantasies.

Whores and Americana

For all the stringencies exercised by the "Puritan ethic," America has always had a soft spot in its history and art for the ladies of horizontal pleasure.

From Dreiser through Capote, our literature is dotted with more-or-less unabashed paeans to the services and personalities of glamorous whores. As often as not, the girls and madams are portrayed as rough-and-tumble creatures of easy virtues but solid hearts. And, outside of fiction, real-life accounts of ex-prostitutes and madams have held a solid sway over the interests of the reading public. Polly Adler, the fun-and-games proprietress of New York's best known bordello during the '20s and '30s, scored a success with her best-seller, *A House Is Not a Home.* And speaking of Miss Adler, her establishment was a favorite haunt of George S. Kaufman, the hypochondriacal playwright who was able to overcome his fastidiousness to the point where he enjoyed a monthly charge account at Adler's. Those were the golden days of whoredom.

Our national myth, too, has been heavily influenced by the accounts of great prostitutes and greater houses. Surely the queen of all brothels was the 50-room mansion maintained in Chicago at the turn of the century by the winsome Everleigh sisters, Ada and Minna. So lavish was their establishment that guests could enjoy the amenities of champagne suppers and music recitals played on a gold-leafed piano.

And, of course, what self-respecting frontier town would allow itself to be caught with its pants down by not offering an accommodating bordello? Whores and gun-slingers are as much a part of the lore of the West as the forty-niners and the sourdoughs.

Hollywood has oiled the dream-machine with whoring epics such as *The Revolt of Mamie Stover, Sadie Thompson, A Walk on the Wild Side, The Owl and the Pussycat*

Exploding the Myth

In real life, there is nothing glamorous about prostitution. It is a terrifying existence of pimps and cops, of scared young girls and callous "johns," the trade sobriquet for the patrons of prostitutes.

Lorrie X. is a 17-year-old prostitute in Washington, D.C. Even at this age, she is a street "pro" with three years' experience. That means she turned her first "trick" when she was fourteen. She is black and services customers in the Southwest ghetto where she was raised. Her first sexual experience was at age 12 when she was raped by an uncle.

It would be comforting to think that 17-year-old Lorrie was an exception. She is not. She is but one of hundreds—perhaps, thousands—of young girls who exist today in what is a true white-slavery trade. The problem is so vast that vice squads are at a loss as to how to stem the traffic.

Runaways are frequent targets for the pimps and assorted panders. Scared, broke, a long way from home, the girls are literally trapped into prostitution by the inducement of drugs, money, and roofs over their heads. In New York City, there have been cases of runaway girls being kidnapped as they stepped off the buses at the sprawling Port Authority bus terminal!

Since accurate records cannot be kept on such a sub-rosa activity as white slavery, it is impossible to estimate how many runaway girls listed on missing-person dossiers across the country are engaged in prostitution. Certainly, from arrest reports alone, the figures are staggeringly high—perhaps more than 200 in New York City. Percentages are equally grim in Washington, Chicago, Los Angeles, and San Francisco.

Not only are the girls becoming prostitutes, but they're becoming desperately vicious as well. In New York, they have taken to cruising in cars and mugging unsuspecting "johns" as they walk the streets. Recently, two hookers accosted a foreign diplomat in front of the New York Hilton and fatally stabbed him.

New York's East Village, the quiet haven of the Flower Children of the early '60s, has turned into a sinkhole of depravity and crime surpassing any of the legendary flesh-pits of the Middle East. The girls come from Dubuque and Kansas City, Terre Haute and Denver. They have no place to go, no money, no friends. They're afraid to call home for fear of parental reprisals, so they drift to the East Village. There the promise of easy drugs and quick money lures them into dead-end streets of prostitution, disease, muggings, and all too frequently, death.

For years, prostitution in the United States was in the hands of hard-bitten professionals: women who had made the conscious decision to sell their bodies for one reason or another. Now, the part-time hookers, spurred on by drug habits in 80 percent of the cases, walk the streets in desperate search for a "john." When the "john" trade is slow, they frequently resort to robberies and muggings performed, usually, with two or more comrades.

The incidence of veneral disease among "free-lancing" streetwalkers—girls who do not use the services of a pimp or syndicate—is appallingly high. According to a New York doctor who has treated many East Village hookers, "The chance of a girl who works the street by herself having gonorrhea or syphilis is almost 100 percent. There's simply no way they can avoid it. They're usually too 'strung out' to seek medical aid from one of the free clinics and, most of the time, they just don't give a damn. I've had 15-year-old girls tell me that they enjoyed the thought of passing 'clap' on to their tricks. It's a sort of a way of getting even for all the wrongs which they feel have been done to them."

The vagrant girls who come under the "protection" of a pimp fare slightly better in some areas, but their lives remain an unremitting hell. Since most pimps like to build a trade, they are usually somewhat concerned about VD and take precautions to keep their girls "clean." Usually they do not allow the girls to roll the clients. Of course, some pimps are interested in one-time setups only wherein the client is physically coerced, robbed, or blackmailed. There is no way to determine in advance whether or not a pimp is "honest."

Pimps keep their girls in line by three methods: physical threats, drugs, and money. All earnings go to the pimp with the pimp picking up living expenses, furnishing an apartment, and giving the girls limited amounts of pocket money. Woe to the girl who attempts to hold out on her pimp: She is burned with heated coat hangers, her drug supply is terminated, and she may even face death.

The traffic in these young people is one of the saddest chapters in contemporary American history. A massive program of social action on all fronts is needed immediately to eliminate this horror. Few problems cry out for a solution with the urgency of this one. No country can live with itself that allows slavery. And no slavery is more heinous than that which is being practiced in the dark recesses of the metropolitan alleys of our nation. It must end.

Starting Time		Finishing Time	
Reading Time		Reading Rate	
Comprehension		Vocabulary	

Comprehension— Read the following questions and statements. For each one, put an *x* in the box before the option that contains the most complete or accurate answer. Check your answers in the Answer Key on page 106.

1. Which of the following are easy victims of white slavery?
   □ a. runaway girls
   □ b. East Village hookers
   □ c. glamorous girls
   □ d. young amateur prostitutes

2. Traditionally, America's attitude toward prostitution has been
   □ a. restrained.
   □ b. critical.
   □ c. enthusiastic.
   □ d. tolerant.

3. Free-lance prostitution goes hand in hand with
   □ a. blackmail.
   □ b. venereal disease.
   □ c. child abuse.
   □ d. law enforcement.

4. A relationship seems to exist between prostitution and
   □ a. glamour.
   □ b. social background.
   □ c. poverty.
   □ d. native intelligence.

5. The selection ends with an appeal for
   □ a. higher morals.
   □ b. legalizing prostitution.
   □ c. police protection.
   □ d. positive action.

6. Many runaways would be better off
   □ a. going to larger cities.
   □ b. frequenting bus stations.
   □ c. staying at home.
   □ d. becoming free-lance prostitutes.

7. Judging by the number of people engaged in prostitution, it can be inferred that it is
   □ a. controllable.   □ c. legal.
   □ b. lucrative.   □ d. ethical.

8. The sentence, "And, of course, what self-respecting frontier town would allow itself to be caught with its pants down by not offering an accommodating bordello?" is meant to be
   □ a. ironic.
   □ b. sarcastic.
   □ c. self-deprecating.
   □ d. good-natured.

9. Most prostitutes sell their bodies because they
   □ a. are looking for fun and adventure.
   □ b. feel they have no other options.
   □ c. want to run their own business.
   □ d. are afraid of disease.

10. The selection is written in the form of
    □ a. an exposition.
    □ b. a review.
    □ c. an interview.
    □ d. a documentary.

Comprehension Skills

1. recalling specific facts	6. making a judgment
2. retaining concepts	7. making an inference
3. organizing facts	8. recognizing tone
4. understanding the main idea	9. understanding characters
5. drawing a conclusion	10. appreciation of literary forms

Study Skills, Part One—Following is a passage with blanks where words have been omitted. Next to the passage are groups of five words, one group for each blank. Complete the passage by selecting the correct word for each of the blanks.

Editing Your Work, II

Make sure to check every sentence. Many problems in a theme or essay may be found in the sentence structure.

3. Check Punctuation. Punctuation is intended to help the reader understand your writing. It is a way of showing on paper the pauses and inflections we make when we __(1)__ .

4. Check Pronouns. Pronouns replace nouns. The antecedent to every pronoun must be __(2)__ to the reader. There should be no doubt what every "it," "he," "they," or "him" refers to.

Check, too, to be sure that each pronoun agrees with its antecedent in person and __(3)__ . A frequent error is to use a plural pronoun (these, they) to replace a singular noun.

5. Improve Nouns and Verbs. Many times a writer will use the same nouns and verbs over and over. This makes the writing dull and unimaginative. Try to __(4)__ each important noun and verb in your paper with a more specific and expressive word. Help the reader see and feel your thoughts. However, avoid __(5)__ or over-inflated language. The object is to produce impact, not poetry.

6. Add Adjectives. Sometimes sentences can be improved by adding a colorful adjective. Try it; it often works. Practice doing this with simple sentences, and see how interesting they can become. This one __(6)__ can double the effectiveness of your writing. But be careful; sometimes a simple, unadorned statement is best, depending on the __(7)__ you are trying to create.

(1)	write		speak
	learn	study	read
(2)	familiar		unknown
	clear	vague	available
(3)	intention		location
	attitude	number	approach
(4)	reverse		improve
	emphasize	replace	restrict
(5)	artificial		realistic
	compact	foreign	familiar
(6)	mistake		description
	purpose	technique	problem
(7)	opportunity		audience
	situation	effort	effect

Study Skills, Part Two—Read the study skills passage again, paying special attention to the lesson being taught. Then, without looking back at the passage, complete each sentence below by writing in the missing word or words. Check the Answer Key on page 106 for the answers to Study Skills, Part One, and Study Skills, Part Two.

1. Punctuation helps the reader to _____ your writing.

2. A frequent error in writing is to use a plural pronoun to replace a _____ noun.

3. Help the reader to see and _____ your thoughts through your writing.

4. Sentences can sometimes be improved by adding a _____ adjective.

5. However, sometimes a _____ , unadorned statement is best.

4 Are You Really Ready for the Highways?

by Norman Richards

Vocabulary—The five words below are from the story you are about to read. Study the words and their meanings. Then complete the ten sentences that follow, using one of the five words to fill in the blank in each sentence. Mark your answer by writing the letter of the word on the line before the sentence. Check your answers in the Answer Key on page 106.

A. refuted: disproved

B. bleaker: drearier; more depressed

C. monotony: tedious sameness

D. spurred: prompted; stimulated

E. mandatory: obligatory

_____ 1. Early critics of superhighways were surprised when their predictions of numerous accidents were _____ .

_____ 2. The _____ of driving on a superhighway can pose a safety hazard.

_____ 3. Outcries from critics have not _____ the government to establish uniform national traffic laws.

_____ 4. For children, playing games can relieve the _____ of long car trips.

_____ 5. Police regularly patrol most sections of superhighways, including the _____ stretches.

_____ 6. Statistics have _____ the notion that superhighway driving is terribly dangerous.

_____ 7. Most safety officials believe that right-hand mirrors should be _____ equipment on all cars.

_____ 8. An increase in accidents has _____ concern over laws which allow passing on the right.

_____ 9. Avoidance of tranquilizers should be _____ for all drivers.

_____ 10. Deserted stretches of superhighways are much _____ than crowded city streets.

My grandfather never drove on a modern interstate superhighway, and he probably would have been scared to death if he had. He would have considered it foolhardy to drive at the dizzying speed of 70 miles an hour with other traffic on the road, and unwise to risk a mechanical breakdown on a bleak highway, miles from help. Yet in the past few decades, due to the greatest road building effort in world history, most Americans have become accustomed to at least an occasional high-speed trip on a freeway, turnpike, or expressway.

Before a long, high-speed trip, check your car—and yourself.

What's more, the gloomy predictions of wholesale highway slaughter by a few early critics have been refuted by national statistics. Superhighways have proved to be safer than ordinary streets and roads. The federal plan for the present network of interstate highways centered on safety as well as speed. The concept of limited access, elimination of traffic lights, division of lanes, and improved grading has eliminated some of the more persistent causes of accidents. But one of the keys to this superior safety record has been driver adaptation to the greater speed and other special conditions of traveling on superhighways.

Superhighway driving *is* different, of course, from the kind of short-haul, in-town driving that most of us do on a daily basis. The average motorist puts a very small percentage of his annual mileage on the high-speed thoroughfare. When he does venture onto them for a vacation trip or other special journey, he's faced with a different set of conditions. How well he adapts to them determines his degree of safe—and pleasurable—traveling.

What are the most common difficulties in adjusting to superhighway driving? What advice do authorities give motorists for better traveling on the high-speed thorough-fares? In seeking the answers to these questions, I talked to state police officers, driver education authorities, members of state highway safety commissions, and officials of the American Automobile Association and the Automobile Legal Association. I also sought advice in the literature available to the motoring public.

Unfortunately, there is a dearth of printed advice on superhighway driving. Automotive magazines, driving school text material, and the literature of many state highway commissions rarely differentiate between the techniques for safe short-haul driving and those required for the expressways and turnpikes. But the authorities with whom I talked were unanimous in their concern that drivers should approach superhighway driving alert to the special demands they impose on driving skills.

"One of the main causes of expressway accidents is slow reflexes," an Illinois state policeman told me. "People just seem to forget they're traveling at much greater speeds on these roads. A driver takes his eyes off the road to light a cigarette or glance at a road map. He looks up again and he's on top of the car in front of him. This is what causes so many tailgate collisions."

Rear-end collisions often occur on highway entrance ramps, too. Have you ever been the second driver on a ramp, waiting to enter the stream of traffic, when the car ahead of you starts to move forward toward the lane of traffic, then stops short? If you had assumed the driver in front of you was going to continue ahead and were looking to your left at the oncoming traffic, you would have hit him.

Plan your trip in advance, say safety authorities. You can save yourself a lot of anxiety and risk if you check a road map before you get on an expressway. Know the number of your exit and the number of miles to it, and have a passenger watch for the exit signs, too. And, of course, if you miss your exit, don't back up, but continue on to the next one and double back.

Most of us are aware of the coordination required to change lanes and pass another car at high speed, but too many drivers neglect to use their directional signals when doing it. Those signals help drivers several car-lengths behind to assess the situation. AAA officials recommend scanning the traffic ahead as far as you can see, rather than keeping your eyes only on the car in front of you. This technique helps drivers avoid getting trapped behind slow-moving vehicles, and it gives them warning of drivers to watch out for: cars that are weaving from lane to lane and ones that straddle the line dividing the lanes.

"Another dangerous, but all-too-common practice," says an Indiana state policeman, "is traveling in the 'blind spot' to the left and behind another car. If the other car changes lanes, there's likely to be an accident. Drivers should get in and out of that blind spot in a hurry when passing."

State highway safety commissions rate fatigue and drowsiness among the most important causes of super-highway accidents. Superhighways have a hypnotic quality and dull the senses during long trips. It's always better to drive in daylight hours when visibility is good, and you're not likely to be tired. Physicians point out that eyestrain is a big factor, too: The glare of oncoming headlights and the limited visibility at night can strain a driver's eyes.

If you're taking any kind of medicine or drugs before an expressway or turnpike trip, you'd do well to check their side effects with your doctor or read the label for warnings. Even such over-the-counter remedies as decongestants and certain cough syrups should be avoided, as well as prolonged use of aspirin. Other obvious medicines to avoid are pep pills and tranquilizers.

Doctors and safety officials warn against eating heavy meals before or during a lengthy trip. They point out that too much food—especially hard-to-digest fried foods like hamburgers and french fries—relaxes, dulls the senses, and causes drowsiness. Soup and frequent light snacks have a better effect and provide all the energy a driver needs. Coffee breaks relieve drowsiness, of course, and one driver training instructor told me he always chews gum on a long trip—it requires him to move his jaws and facial muscles enough to keep him alert. Another important consideration is the frequent circulation of fresh air in the car, even in winter when it may be temporarily uncomfortable.

What about the business of having a breakdown, miles from the nearest service station? Police and highway commissioners are aware of these problems and can even predict the approximate number of breakdowns per year on various highways. "The obvious way to avoid breakdowns is to check the car before starting a trip," says a Missouri state trooper. "Tires are most important. So are brakes, steering, windshield wipers."

Suppose you have checked to be certain your car is in good working order, and you still have a breakdown. There's nothing bleaker than the feeling of being abandoned on a lonely stretch of road with no help in sight. But there's really little cause for alarm. Most highways are well patrolled by police cars and emergency vehicles. Their schedules are arranged so that no stretch of the highway goes unnoticed for a long time.

Police say the important thing to do when a car breaks down is to get it completely off the pavement, even if it means driving on a flat tire for a distance. The standard distress signals in all states, of course, are emergency flasher lights and a raised hood. Drivers without flasher lights should display a white handkerchief on the left side of the car and turn off all lights at night. Safety officials say many a parked car has been hit when an oncoming motorist followed a pair of taillights in the dark without realizing they weren't moving.

On long trips, driver fatigue may loom as one of the greatest dangers. Set realistic mileage goals in advance— 300 to 400 miles a day is considered a safe figure.

Monotony may not be as great a safety menace as fatigue, but if it affects children on a family trip, it can result in frayed nerves and distraction for the driver. To break the monotony, it's good to keep the children's interest alive with games and such.

Although pressure by the federal government has spurred the introduction of automobile safety equipment in recent years, the government has failed in one important safety area: the establishment of uniform national traffic laws. Superhighway drivers should be aware that such practices as passing on the right are legal in some states but not in others. At present, 44 states allow passing on the right on multi-lane highways, but few of them have made it mandatory for cars to be equipped with mirrors on the right side, which most safety experts consider essential.

Some authorities condemn laws that allow passing on the right as a danger to motorists. Philip C. Wallwork, public relations director of the Automobile Legal Association, is one of a growing group who recommends abolishing them.

"We've seen an increasing number of turnpike and expressway accidents where a car bolts across the center strip out of control because the driver was startled by a car suddenly overtaking him on the right," he says. "If the police would make a greater effort to discourage the slow drivers who block the left lanes, there would be no need to allow passing on the right."

Efforts are being made to establish a uniform national system of highway traffic laws, but until this is achieved, the best advice to the motorist is to keep in mind the inconsistencies among state traffic laws and to check the legal regulations before he takes to the superhighways.

Starting Time			*Finishing Time*	
Reading Time			*Reading Rate*	
Comprehension			*Vocabulary*	

Comprehension— Read the following questions and statements. For each one, put an *x* in the box before the option that contains the most complete or accurate answer. Check your answers in the Answer Key on page 106.

1. One of the main causes of highway accidents is
   □ a. high speeds.
   □ b. poor lighting.
   □ c. tailgating.
   □ d. slow reflexes.

2. Superhighways are safer than ordinary streets and roads because they are
   □ a. faster.
   □ b. well designed.
   □ c. well traveled.
   □ d. patrolled.

3. If you eat a heavy meal before driving, you are likely to
   ☐ a. stay alert.   ☐ c. drive faster.
   ☐ b. become drowsy.   ☐ d. become jumpy.

4. Safe driving on superhighways requires
   ☐ a. some adjustments from ordinary in-town driving.
   ☐ b. national traffic laws.
   ☐ c. less skill than driving in heavy city traffic.
   ☐ d. extra car maintenance.

5. The best way to reduce fatigue on a long trip is to
   ☐ a. keep your eyes on the road.
   ☐ b. make frequent lane changes.
   ☐ c. break the trip up into manageable segments.
   ☐ d. avoid all food and drink while driving.

6. Superhighways have proven to be
   ☐ a. a menace to public safety.
   ☐ b. a safe and efficient means of travel.
   ☐ c. inordinately expensive and difficult to maintain.
   ☐ d. damaging to vehicles and their drivers.

7. It can be inferred from the selection that highway travel
   ☐ a. should not be taken lightly.
   ☐ b. should not be attempted by young, inexperienced drivers.
   ☐ c. requires highly trained motorists.
   ☐ d. should be avoided whenever possible.

8. The tone of the selection is
   ☐ a. frightening.
   ☐ b. factual.
   ☐ c. threatening.
   ☐ d. negative.

9. The police officers mentioned in this selection are
   ☐ a. dedicated and concerned.
   ☐ b. overworked and irritable.
   ☐ c. rude and thoughtless.
   ☐ d. worried and afraid.

10. The expression "scared to death" is
   ☐ a. a symbol.
   ☐ b. an allusion.
   ☐ c. an overstatement.
   ☐ d. a metaphor.

Comprehension Skills

1. recalling specific facts	6. making a judgment
2. retaining concepts	7. making an inference
3. organizing facts	8. recognizing tone
4. understanding the main idea	9. understanding characters
5. drawing a conclusion	10. appreciation of literary forms

Study Skills, Part One—Following is a passage with blanks where words have been omitted. Next to the passage are groups of five words, one group for each blank. Complete the passage by selecting the correct word for each of the blanks.

Editing Your Work, III

7. Use Appropriate Language. There are, as you know, levels of language usage. Formal occasions demand the use of formal language, while conversations with friends permit the use of fragmented, informal speech. The language you use must be ___(1)___ for your subject, purpose, and reader.

ANALYZE OTHER WRITING

The final bit of advice we can pass along to developing writers is to ___(2)___ the writings of others. By others, we refer, of course, to published authors and professional writers.

Most composition courses include the use of readers. These are books containing ___(3)___ kinds and styles of writing for students to analyze and imitate. The selections in the reader are designed to serve as ___(4)___ for you.

Take a paragraph or two from an effective piece of writing and study it. Judge each sentence against the

(1)	suitable	difficult	
	challenging	reasonable	unfit
(2)	ignore	study	
	copy	adapt	criticize
(3)	matching	different	
	similar	identical	opposite
(4)	models	sources	
	compositions	warnings	drawings

suggestions presented above for editing your work. Especially notice the nouns and __(5)__ . Are they specific and image-provoking? They are certain to be in good writing.

Check the adjectives, too. See how experienced writers create word __(6)__ through descriptive terms. Notice how the professionals organize their work and develop every idea.

Writing need not be a chore for you. Try following the suggestions given here, and see if you don't __(7)__ a more expressive and more competent writer.

(5)	conjunctions	interjections
	verbs adverbs	pronouns
(6)	stories	pictures
	sequences combinations	collections
(7)	imitate	envy
	admire dislike	become

Study Skills, Part Two—Read the study skills passage again, paying special attention to the lesson being taught. Then, without looking back at the passage, complete each sentence below by writing in the missing word or words. Check the Answer Key on page 106 for the answers to Study Skills, Part One, and Study Skills, Part Two.

1. Different occasions demand different _____ of language usage.

2. Developing writers should study the work of _____ authors and professional writers.

3. Books known as readers, offered in composition courses, provide styles of writing for students to analyze and _____ .

4. Each sentence of the selections from the reader should be _____ against the suggestions presented for editing the student's own work.

5. Professionals organize their work and _____ every idea.

5 | The Duck Man of Venice

by Skip Ferderber

Vocabulary—The five words below are from the story you are about to read. Study the words and their meanings. Then complete the ten sentences that follow, using one of the five words to fill in the blank in each sentence. Mark your answer by writing the letter of the word on the line before the sentence. Check your answers in the Answer Key on page 106.

A. ill-kempt: disheveled; slovenly

B. anathema: a greatly detested thing

C. sustain: keep in existence; maintain

D. reverberates: echoes

E. incensed: infuriated; angered greatly

_____ 1. Buddy Hayes works hard to _____ the waterfowl near his home.

_____ 2. The streets of Venice, California, are filled with loud, _____ children.

_____ 3. Some neighbors are _____ by the noise Buddy's ducks make at feeding time.

_____ 4. When Buddy Hayes laughs, his voice _____ through his white stucco house.

_____ 5. Ducks need fresh water to _____ themselves.

_____ 6. The idea of slaughtering the canal ducks for food is an _____ to Buddy Hayes.

_____ 7. During botulism attacks, Buddy Hayes's plea for help with the ducks _____ through the neighborhood.

_____ 8. Buddy's dogs become _____ when marauding animals threaten the ducks on their property.

_____ 9. Salt water is _____ to the ducks in the canal.

_____ 10. Venice, California, is a decaying neighborhood dotted with _____ houses.

To several hundred ducks and geese living in the stagnant salty waters which fill the once elegant canals of Venice, California, a roly-poly tuba player has become their benefactor, their doctor—and literally their connection to life itself.

To a visitor to Southern California, the colorful Venice Canals—a sleepy decaying neighborhood located a half-mile from the Pacific Ocean with graffiti-scrawled walls, ill-kempt buildings, long-haired hippies, and an abundance of dirty children who play loudly beside the crumbling seawalls—somehow become more quaint with the constant honking of the waterfowl that have made the old and rundown area their home.

Their charm, however, masks their desperate state. With salt water from the ocean filling the canals being anathema to the freshwater birds; with little or no vegetation to sustain them; and with too many birds and too many hazards such as dogs and cruel human beings, the quackers and honkers are faced with a desperate situation.

It would be far worse without the Duck Man of Venice.

His name is Buddy Hayes, or, more formally, Theodore Hayes. He has taken on the enormously complex job of providing food, water, and medical attention for Venice's troubled waterfowl community.

Twice a day, at 11 A.M. and 5 P.M., the usually quiet neighborhood reverberates with the rasping sound of hundreds of quacking birds who throng and gawk outside the white picket fence surrounding Hayes's two-story house, situated on the corner of a canal intersection.

The ducks, acting like quibbling ladies at a clothing sale, vie for space near where Hayes or his wife, Jean, will offer a smorgasbord of duck pellets, hard corn kernels, lettuce leaves, and other greens.

The door opens and out marches Hayes, a chubby, smiling elf of a man dressed in a gray jumpsuit and poncho, bright red boots, and a wreath of graying hair topped with a pony tail tied with a rubber band.

He approaches the fence, waits for the appropriate moment, and flings the food in a grainy shower. The birds heave to their meal with a vengeance.

And while they eat, Hayes changes their water, providing fresh water for the birds to drink and to bathe in—the only way they have to wash the deathly salt off their feathers, salt which tends to make it increasingly hard for them to fly or to live.

It's been this way seven days a week for the 54-year-old musician, a former regular with the Lawrence Welk ensemble, who views the survival of the ducks as a labor of love—even though the cost of purchasing food, water, and veterinarian services runs over $600 a year, money he can ill afford.

A roly-poly tuba player has become a waterfowl benefactor and doctor.

"It's an unnatural place for the ducks to live," said Hayes one day recently, slouched in a chair, his hands on his potbelly, watching with fondness as his charges loudly gobbled their midday meal. "They're freshwater creatures, not saltwater, and yet people insist on dumping their ducks here in the canals.

"Every year, around Easter especially, we get a lot of ducks, kids having let them go in the canals after getting them for gifts and getting tired of them real fast.

"And they start multiplying and, well, you know, here they are." He looked thoughtful for a moment. "I sure wish these pet-shop owners would stop selling them. Maybe some of them don't know that the animals they sell are going to wind up down here. I don't know. . . ."

When he came to the canals following a long career as a tuba player, a bass player, and a comedian, he bought a house and began the process of transforming it into a delightful two-story local landmark with a gray-painted roof, white stucco, and red trimming.

After years of traveling with bands—including Welk's and at one time, his own—it was time to settle down and enjoy life.

He reckoned, however, without the ducks.

"It was about the time I moved here that I noticed the ducks starting to come," he reminisced. "I began feeding them along with some others in the neighborhood. I'm about the only one left, I guess."

He also converted an empty lot adjacent to his house into a duck shelter and hospital for birds injured by overexposure to salt water or that have been injured by neighborhood dogs and cats.

Over the years, Hayes has pulled through dozens of the waterfowl by providing a recuperation area and by footing expensive veterinarian bills. He is not sure exactly how high the bills are: "I don't dare look at them," he winces.

Aside from the natural dangers, which have included a severe botulism attack, he faces the duck's own reproductive cycle, a problem which continues to create an overpopulation problem in the canals.

On occasion, he has enlisted the help of sympathetic young people who have combed the canal banks for birds' nests, breaking any eggs they found. But he is not always too successful, and the results are tragic when he is not.

"Not too long ago," he said, "I picked up ten baby geese and raised them in my backyard. I released them and it was only a couple of days later that I looked out into the canal near my backyard and found five of them dead, floating in the water. So I got the other five and I've got them here in my backyard. I don't know what I'm going to do with them."

One solution he tried was to give them away to Hollywood Park, one of Southern California's largest racetracks which features an infield area with an extensive waterfowl collection. The park shied away from any outside donations, other than those arranged by the waterfowl manager. Hayes is still looking for some people who would like to become foster parents to the geese.

The ducks and geese are also easy prey to neighborhood pets. To prevent this, Hayes has planted heavy shrubbery around his property in an effort to ward off any marauding dogs and cats. His three dogs, in addition, have voluntarily taken over the job of "watchdog" for the ducks. "Whenever the ducks quack a sort of a warning signal, a sound that the dogs recognize, they'll go over and help to chase intruders off the property."

One danger that he has little control over is the most dangerous animal of all: man. "The street people eat them once in a while," he said, shaking his head sadly. "I've never seen anyone actually picking up any of the ducks, but every so often I'll see something in a trash can that looks suspiciously like duck feathers."

He added that he didn't think they would be good eating: "With all the salt water they've drunk, the meat is probably too salty."

Another problem facing the Duck Man of Venice is a massive reconstruction of the canals, financed by property owners by assessments to the tune of $24.5 million, and which will include draining of the canals. Although the starting date may be years away, owing to a series of lawsuits, Hayes still feels obligated to try to make some sort of arrangements for the birds.

"If the draining of the canals doesn't get them," he said, "the dogs will. I'm just going to try to keep them alive until the project starts and take them somewhere else so they'll have some sort of protection.

"They can't go and join their fellow birds because most of them are domesticated and they don't know how to fly."

Over the years, he has received complaints from some neighbors who become incensed by the rat-tat-tat sound of a gaggle of geese and ducks calling for their food. Hayes threw up his hands. "You know, they were really the ones who helped encourage the ducks. They started putting out food and water and the ducks multiplied and then the people stopped and the ducks were still here."

He has asked for cooperation from the city of Los Angeles—Venice being a suburb of the megalopolis—but he has received little help. According to his wife, Jean, the city was asked to transport some of the ducks elsewhere to avoid overcrowding and to lessen the chance of a botulism epidemic—an ever-current possibility with the presence of even one duck infected with the killer disease.

But waterfowl, she explained, are under the control of the state fish and game commission and the city apparently has been unable to make arrangements to transport the ducks. "They can't place them locally because every place around here is loaded with ducks," she said.

While the Hayeses have been the ducks' chief supporters, they hasten to add that some of the long-haired young people in the neighborhood have eagerly responded to help care for the ducks when help has been requested, especially during a botulism attack.

But by and large, the main responsibility still falls on Buddy Hayes. And he does not shirk that task. Even though his current job—playing in a downtown Los Angeles dance ballroom four nights a week—pays him a somewhat limited wage, and even though he faces paying a hefty assessment on his property as a result of the canals reconstruction project, he is determined to do what he can for as long as he can.

"As long as I have a dime in my pocket," said Hayes with a gleam in his eye, "I'll feed the ducks. I might lose my house"—and he laughed—"but I'll feed the ducks."

Starting Time		Finishing Time	
Reading Time		Reading Rate	
Comprehension		Vocabulary	

Comprehension— Read the following questions and statements. For each one, put an x in the box before the option that contains the most complete or accurate answer. Check your answers in the Answer Key on page 106.

1. In the vacant lot next to his house, Buddy Hayes set up
   - ☐ a. a duck shelter and hospital.
   - ☐ b. a shelter for local street people.
   - ☐ c. breeding grounds for ducks from the canal.
   - ☐ d. a petting farm where local children can play with the ducks.

2. The future of Buddy Hayes's ducks is
   - ☐ a. uncertain.
   - ☐ b. encouraging.
   - ☐ c. bright.
   - ☐ d. destruction.

3. Buddy Hayes became concerned about the fate of the canal ducks
   - □ a. when he was still a child.
   - □ b. while touring with the Lawrence Welk orchestra.
   - □ c. during the first botulism epidemic to hit the canals.
   - □ d. only after moving to Venice.

4. Which of the following expresses the attitude behind Buddy Hayes's efforts?
   - □ a. All life is precious.
   - □ b. Recognition takes time.
   - □ c. Children are cruel.
   - □ d. Government is uncaring.

5. The ducks in the Venice canals are mostly
   - □ a. the multicolored wild species.
   - □ b. the sea-going variety.
   - □ c. prized for their tasty meat.
   - □ d. the common white variety.

6. The duck problem in the Venice canals could be reduced and possibly solved by
   - □ a. an organized effort to educate people.
   - □ b. a ban on the sale of ducks in pet shops.
   - □ c. pumping fresh water into the canals.
   - □ d. following the example of Buddy Hayes.

7. It can be inferred from the selection that
   - □ a. Californians are cruel to wildlife.
   - □ b. the ducks cannot adapt to conditions in the canal.
   - □ c. long-haired hippies spoiled the once elegant canals.
   - □ d. the canals cannot be improved.

8. When Buddy Hayes says, "I sure wish these pet-shop owners would stop selling [ducks]. Maybe some of them don't know that the animals they sell are going to wind up down here. I don't know. . . .", he is speaking
   - □ a. sarcastically.
   - □ b. blithely.
   - □ c. cynically.
   - □ d. wistfully.

9. Buddy Hayes and his wife Jean are
   - □ a. inconsistent.
   - □ b. compassionate.
   - □ c. bothersome.
   - □ d. headstrong.

10. The selection is written in the form of
   - □ a. a report.
   - □ b. an interview.
   - □ c. an open letter.
   - □ d. an editorial.

Comprehension Skills

1. recalling specific facts	6. making a judgment
2. retaining concepts	7. making an inference
3. organizing facts	8. recognizing tone
4. understanding the main idea	9. understanding characters
5. drawing a conclusion	10. appreciation of literary forms

Study Skills, Part One

Study Skills, Part One—Following is a passage with blanks where words have been omitted. Next to the passage are groups of five words, one group for each blank. Complete the passage by selecting the correct word for each of the blanks.

The Art of Writing, I

It seems that many students distinctly dislike writing although reading, writing, and speaking are the student's ___(1)___ of learning. We all have good ideas—the trouble arises in ___(2)___ our ideas. It is the lack of organization that makes students fear writing. The student who can organize his approach to writing will find the experience rewarding if not enjoyable.

Here are the steps to follow when preparing to write.

STATE A SUBJECT

You must think first and carefully about your ___(3)___ . It should not be just a one-word title; it should be a statement of the topic you plan to discuss and it should

(1)	method		idea
	plan	system	tools
(2)		expressing	organizing
	utilizing	memorizing	understanding
(3)		character	paragraph
	sentence	subject	word

also state what you plan to say about it. You should be able to state clearly in a sentence or two the views you wish to present relating to your subject. Many students fail before they even begin by not ___(4)___ what their views are. Obviously, you cannot write ___(5)___ if you don't know what you're going to say; yet, how many times have you attempted to do just this? Spend enough time forming your subject statement; it saves you time later.

LIMIT THE SUBJECT

You should know before you begin writing how ___(6)___ your paper will be, or how long you want it to be. This means that your subject will have to be limited to just those aspects that can be suitably reported in a paper of that length. Many students try to include too much in too little space. The result is that they have not really covered anything—their paper consists of a series of ___(7)___ general facts with no real point or substance.

You must stop, think, and define the limitations of your subject. Decide exactly on the two or three points you want to consider and know before you write what you intend to say about them.

(4)   understanding   determining
       illustrating   describing   presenting

(5)   interestingly   sufficiently
       seriously   effectively   exclusively

(6)   long   interesting
       exciting   boring   complete

(7)   related   unrelated
       unusually   ordinary   understandable

Study Skills, Part Two—Read the study skills passage again, paying special attention to the lesson being taught. Then, without looking back at the passage, complete each sentence below by writing in the missing word or words. Check the Answer Key on page 106. for the answers to Study Skills, Part One, and Study Skills, Part Two.

1. It is the lack of _____ that makes students fear writing.

2. The student who can organize his _____ to writing will find the experience rewarding.

3. You should be able to state clearly, in a sentence or two, the _____ you wish to present relating to your subject.

4. Spend enough time forming your subject _____ ; it saves you time later.

5. You must stop, think, and define the _____ of your subject.

Vocabulary—The five words below are from the story you are about to read. Study the words and their meanings. Then complete the ten sentences that follow, using one of the five words to fill in the blank in each sentence. Mark your answer by writing the letter of the word on the line before the sentence. Check your answers in the Answer Key on page 106.

A. formidable: awesome; dreaded

B. habitats: natural environments

C. propensity: tendency

D. inevitable: unavoidable

E. replete: very full; abundant

_____ 1. Human expansion has destroyed the _____ of some species.

_____ 2. Americans have shown a _____ to help the underdog.

_____ 3. The destruction of a species' _____ can lead to its extinction.

_____ 4. The endangered species list drawn up by the U.S. Department of the Interior is _____ with species which may soon disappear from the earth.

_____ 5. Extinction of the bison no longer seems _____ .

_____ 6. Many _____ creatures that once roamed this planet have long since become extinct.

_____ 7. As pollution levels increase, it is _____ that more and more species will be affected.

_____ 8. Some people have a _____ to put a price tag on everything, even the wonders of nature.

_____ 9. The world is _____ with fascinating mammals, birds, fish, reptiles, and amphibians.

_____ 10. Advancing glaciers were among the _____ obstacles faced by ancient animals.

A little more than a century ago a man could watch by the hour as millions of passenger pigeons winged overhead, literally shutting out the sun.

A little more than a half a century ago the last passenger pigeon on earth died in a zoo.

A little more than a century ago a man might have watched by the hour as a herd of bison thundered across the land.

What causes a species to become extinct? What's being done to protect our endangered wildlife?

A little more than half a century ago the American bison had been reduced to a few hundred stragglers. But a spark of concern caught fire, and the bison was brought back from the edge of oblivion to continue as part of America's wildlife heritage.

Today the future of many kinds of wildlife depends on how brightly burns that spark of concern. We can recall, in shortened form, Aldo Leopold's observation on the extinction of the passenger pigeon: "For one species to mourn the death of another is a new thing under the sun. We, who have lost our pigeons, mourn the loss. Had the funeral been ours, the pigeons would hardly have mourned us. In this fact, rather than in nylons or atomic bombs, lies evidence of our superiority over the beasts." And we can be assured by the bison we see today that imperiled wildlife can be saved when concern is bright enough.

Through the eons of time, who knows how many kinds of animals have lived and died? Why did the huge dinosaurs, the formidable saber-toothed tiger, the diminutive four-toed horse, the gigantic mastodons and mammoths disappear from the earth? They held important places in the wildlife communities of their times, which collectively spanned millions of years. Now they are known only from fossils in the crust of the earth.

These ancient species disappeared along with thousands of others that lived long before man began to dominate the earth. We can only speculate on the cause of their demise on the basis of geologic evidence and our knowledge of species that survived until historic times.

Our wild animals have developed through natural selective processes. Each different form has special characteristics, unique features that have enabled it to survive. These attributes fit them for specific niches in their environment. If species arise that are better adapted to fill community niches, the original occupants are replaced, and when there is an adverse change in the conditions for which a species is fitted, it faces two alternatives: Adapt or perish.

Before the arrival of man, species disappeared because of gradual climatic changes, glacial advances, or inundation by ancient seas. These changes eliminated or adversely modified their habitats. Some lost out in their fight for life when competition with other species grew too intense.

Changes have been speeded up by civilized man with his technological means of rapidly altering the environment, his propensity for introducing competing species, both wild and domestic, and his more direct means of destruction. As a result, species are now disappearing faster than they are evolving.

What Makes a Species Become Extinct?

How can you tell if an animal is in jeopardy? To determine whether a species is in danger, information is needed about the area it originally occupied and its abundance, the changes in its distribution and the causes of those changes, its present status in numbers and range, and the natural and human factors that may act upon it. We need to know when pollution may be making unlivable the only stream that is the habitat of a race of fish; or when the drying up of the last bit of marsh will wipe out the only source of food or nesting cover for a species of bird; or when expansion by another species will bring about, through interbreeding, the disappearance of the special characteristics that distinguish an interesting subspecies.

Specialists at the Bureau of Sport Fisheries and Wildlife of the U.S. Department of the Interior have suggested the circumstances under which wildlife should be considered in peril and have prepared a list of those considered rare and endangered. The terms used to show the status of wildlife species and subspecies or races are these:

An *endangered* form is one whose prospects of survival and reproduction are in immediate jeopardy. Its peril may result from one or many causes—ravages of disease, predation by other animals, competition from a more aggressive species, or changes in and loss of habitat. Endangered animals must have help, or extinction will probably soon follow. In this classification are about 90 mammals, birds, fish, reptiles, and amphibians.

A *rare* form is one whose numbers are few throughout its range. So long as conditions remain stable and favorable, such species may continue to survive in limited numbers. When such an animal occupies a limited habitat, adverse influences are more critical, and unfavorable changes in its environment may quickly make it endangered. In this classification are nearly 45 mammals, birds, fish, reptiles, and amphibians.

In addition there are *peripheral* forms whose occurrence in the United States is at the edge of their natural range. Such an animal may be found in satisfactory numbers outside our country, but its retention in our nation's fauna may call for special attention. In this classification the specialists note over 80 mammals, birds, fish, and reptiles.

In *status undetermined* have been placed over 100 mammals, birds, and fish. Biologists have suggested that information be sought on these so that their status can be determined. Some of them may be in danger.

Education

Universal stewardship of wildlife should be a national objective. Responsible citizens must not only obey the laws themselves but must encourage others to obey. Organizations and individuals who have an interest in our native wildlife must take every opportunity to convey the conservation message to everyone. The subject is front-page news. Interesting articles and pictures are readily accepted by the press and they form the basis for popular television programs.

Practically untouched are the opportunities for bringing this conservation message to schoolchildren. The story of endangered wildlife is the chronicle of much of our wasted natural wealth, though wildlife not yet extinct is a renewable resource.

The Price is Right

There is even an economic advantage to the perpetuation of endangered animals. Concentrations of wildlife of any kind seem to draw people: Chambers of Commerce often advertise them as local attractions. When people gather, they naturally spend money and prime the local economy. Curiosity draws thousands of visitors to Aransas National Wildlife Refuge in Texas, where the few remaining magnificent whooping cranes gather to spend the winter. Sightseeing boats on the Intracoastal Waterway near the refuge enable people to get a view of these majestic birds. But in our whole national economy this is only a small part.

Many animals whose existence is in jeopardy were once important sources of food or other raw material for human use. The bison and the beaver practically supported the exploration and initial settlement of the West. The passenger pigeon, the sturgeon, and the prairie chicken were staple food items in the markets of yesteryear. Prairie chickens are unlikely to become an important food item again, but the fur seal and the northern sea-otter herds have been rescued from the brink of extinction to become important items of commerce.

Americans are notorious for their interest in the underdog. This interest goes out to wildlife struggling for their very existence against obstacles that sometimes are the inevitable results of human progress, but may also be the results of human indifference or greed.

Suppose the last whooping crane quietly gave up the struggle for survival in some lonely marsh. Would it make any difference to you? Chances are you'll never see a live one anyhow—millions of Americans never will. Why worry? The same may be said of many other rare or endangered species. What are the values of these creatures? Why spend time and effort to save them?

Worth the Effort

Coldly appraised, there is little doubt we could get along without most forms of wildlife, be they common, rare, or threatened with extinction. We could get along without baseball or golf or automobiles or many, many other things—if we had to. But each of these helps make life easier or more pleasant or more interesting. It's a question of how many good things we want and can afford.

A businessman, after a period of tense competition, realized he must either slow up or blow up and took off on a fishing trip to the coast. The three game fish he caught were big ones, and figuring what he had spent for his trip, they had a value of about $170 apiece. Or was that the value of the fish?

Can we set a value on a whooping crane as the price a zoo might offer on a free and open market?

The American bison or buffalo has been restored to the point that it is necessary to keep some of the herds to manageable size by disposing of a few animals for food. Should we figure the true worth of bison to the American people in food-store values?

Can the worth of a city park be calculated in board feet of trees and cubic feet of soil? Or in children's feet at play?

A generation ago there was a vogue for estimating the worth of the chemicals and other elements that make up a human's body. In those days it came to something less than a dollar. Prices are higher now and no doubt a human these days is worth more than a dollar. Isn't he?

Why feel concern for whooping cranes?

History is replete with examples of evolution and change, a matter of considerable import to mankind as an indication or insight into his own future. Threatened forms are visible indicators of some of the changes that are continually occurring but often so subtly as to be otherwise unnoticed and therefore unmeasured.

Man's wisdom and experience have not been extensive enough to grasp the full significance of the loss of a species of wildlife. Each occupies a niche and makes a contribution to the whole of life. The biological impact of forever removing a form from the environment may not always be readily discernible, but something of value has been lost.

Human happiness is the sum total of all the desires and enjoyments and accomplishments of all the individuals who make up the human population. Take one part from the whole and it is no longer complete.

As the numbers of our wildlife grow fewer, their true individual value grows greater, for in the few are concentrated all the worth of one small but valuable part of our whole world.

Starting Time		Finishing Time	
Reading Time		Reading Rate	
Comprehension		Vocabulary	

Comprehension — Read the following questions and statements. For each one, put an *x* in the box before the option that contains the most complete or accurate answer. Check your answers in the Answer Key on page 106.

1. It was public concern that saved the bison from extinction. The strength of this concern will
   - ☐ a. encourage the creation of many parks and zoos.
   - ☐ b. determine the future of many kinds of wildlife.
   - ☐ c. limit the great industrial productivity of America.
   - ☐ d. interfere with the survival of small animal species.

2. Species are presently disappearing faster than they are evolving because of
   - ☐ a. natural disasters.
   - ☐ b. diminishing funds.
   - ☐ c. population control.
   - ☐ d. human technology.

3. By the time a species is placed on the endangered species list, it is
   - ☐ a. too late to save it.
   - ☐ b. in immediate danger of becoming extinct.
   - ☐ c. suffering from the ravages of disease.
   - ☐ d. of great interest to all types of tourists.

4. Aldo Leopold's observation can be interpreted to mean which of the following?
   - ☐ a. Man should concentrate solely on his own survival.
   - ☐ b. Man should take pride in his humanity.
   - ☐ c. Technological progress determines man's basic superiority.
   - ☐ d. Pigeons are unworthy of man's concern.

5. Forms of wildlife which require immediate help are those which are classified as
   - ☐ a. endangered.
   - ☐ b. rare.
   - ☐ c. peripheral.
   - ☐ d. status undetermined.

6. The ultimate responsibility for the preservation of wildlife lies with
   - ☐ a. the federal government.
   - ☐ b. the public media.
   - ☐ c. the general public.
   - ☐ d. concerned groups.

7. The extinction of the dinosaur and the saber-toothed tiger suggests that
   - ☐ a. they failed to adapt.
   - ☐ b. man destroyed their environment.
   - ☐ c. they became too numerous.
   - ☐ d. pollution was not controlled.

8. The author treats the notion that a human body is only worth a dollar or so as
   - ☐ a. illogical.
   - ☐ b. accurate.
   - ☐ c. mystifying.
   - ☐ d. superficial.

9. The people who saved the bison from extinction were
   - ☐ a. greedy.
   - ☐ b. short-sighted.
   - ☐ c. noble.
   - ☐ d. misguided.

10. The selection is written in the form of a
   - ☐ a. thesis.
   - ☐ b. report.
   - ☐ c. debate.
   - ☐ d. story.

Comprehension Skills

1. recalling specific facts	6. making a judgment
2. retaining concepts	7. making an inference
3. organizing facts	8. recognizing tone
4. understanding the main idea	9. understanding characters
5. drawing a conclusion	10. appreciation of literary forms

Study Skills, Part One — Following is a passage with blanks where words have been omitted. Next to the passage are groups of five words, one group for each blank. Complete the passage by selecting the correct word for each of the blanks.

The Art of Writing, II

We have said that the first two tasks for the writer are (1) select a subject, and (2) limit the subject. Here are the next steps for the student to take.

CLARIFY THE PURPOSE

Every student has a ___(1)___ in mind when writing. It may be the purpose assigned by the instructor or, too often,

(1)   situation   purpose
       character   definition   problem

it may be some vague, poorly defined idea of what the student hopes to accomplish.

Words should convey the exact (2) intended by the writer. This presupposes that the writer knows which exact meaning he wants to convey. This must be part of the plan; the writer must know clearly what his purpose in writing is: a position must be taken regarding the subject and the writer must defend or support it. Purposeless writing is (3) writing. Unless the reader knows where you are leading him, your writing will not make sense. Aimless writing creates aimless and dull reading. Be sure of your stand before beginning to write.

SUPPORT THE IDEAS

Every paper, essay, or theme must do more than merely present facts: the facts must be (4) . A writer cannot expect readers to accept a particular position unless it is properly presented and clearly (5) .

This does not mean that everything you write has to take a stand on some controversial issue—it means that, whatever the subject and purpose, your writing must include the facts, details, and illustrations that make your ideas reasonable and acceptable to the reader.

There are, of course, various patterns of (6) used by authors. As you read and study, take ideas from these patterns. Employ the different (7) shown in these patterns in your own writing. Observe how skilled writers flood the reader with all kinds of support for their generalizations and main ideas.

(2)		
sentence		paragraph
occasion	illustration	meaning

(3)		
ineffective		interesting
effective	successful	distracting

(4)		
suppressed		discussed
supported	retracted	described

(5)		
punctuated		printed
determined	questioned	defined

(6)		
adjustment		involvement
development	influence	enjoyment

(7)		
techniques		paragraphs
attitudes	presentations	chapters

Study Skills, Part Two—Read the study skills passage again, paying special attention to the lesson being taught. Then, without looking back at the passage, complete each sentence below by writing in the missing word or words. Check the Answer Key on page 106 for the answers to Study Skills, Part One, and Study Skills, Part Two.

1. The first two tasks of the writer are to _____ a subject and to limit the subject.

2. The writer must take a _____ regarding his subject and must defend or support it.

3. Unless the reader knows where you are leading him, your writing will not make _____ .

4. Every paper or theme must do more than merely present _____ .

5. Your writing must include facts, details, and illustrations that make your ideas reasonable and _____ to the reader.

7 | Dr. Batman

by Anthony Wolff

Vocabulary—The five words below are from the story you are about to read. Study the words and their meanings. Then complete the ten sentences that follow, using one of the five words to fill in the blank in each sentence. Mark your answer by writing the letter of the word on the line before the sentence. Check your answers in the Answer Key on page 107.

A. frequent: to go to or visit often

B. ingenuity: cleverness

C. validating: proving; verifying

D. hypothesis: theory

E. impregnated: filled; saturated

_____ 1. Hundreds of thousands of bats _____ a single cave in Eagle Creek Canyon.

_____ 2. Dr. Petit has shown great _____ in searching out caves where bats dwell.

_____ 3. So far Dr. Petit's results support his original _____ .

_____ 4. The presence of mercury wastes in Eagle Creek bat guano helps in _____ Dr. Petit's theories.

_____ 5. The bat droppings are _____ with all the environmental poisons in the surrounding region.

_____ 6. Dr. Petit's perseverance and _____ may lead to important findings.

_____ 7. Aid from the Rockefeller Foundation allows Dr. Petit to test his _____ .

_____ 8. The well-known history of a nearby copper smelter was helpful in _____ Dr. Petit's measurements of Eagle Creek bat guano.

_____ 9. After paraffin has _____ a sample of bat guano, the sample can be analyzed without fear of it crumbling.

_____ 10. Most people do not _____ bat caves.

In most folk, a fascination with bats might be thought morbid. Bats, after all, are bizarre creatures: dog-faced, bird-winged mammals that frequent the night. Count Dracula's mythic consorts, they still inspire nightmare sleep and waking fear in normal folk. But for Dr. Michael Petit, a sane, sociable microbiologist at Colorado State University

A Colorado microbiologist studies the stratified evidence of environmental misuse in an unusual material.

in Fort Collins, bats are a professional obsession. With modest support from the Rockefeller Foundation, he pursues them throughout the Southwest, from Colorado to Mexico.

In fact, it is not the bats themselves that fascinate Dr. Petit, though he likes them well enough. His special interest is reserved for what the bats leave behind in their dark, isolated caves. Each year—generation after generation, sometimes for centuries—the migratory bat colonies carpet the floors of their summer homes with droppings (known politely as "guano," from the Spanish), as well as with corpses and other souvenirs. In that accumulated debris, Dr. Petit is seeking an index to the past. The bats' leavings contain traces of various environmental poisons—mercury, lead, etc.—that the mammals have ingested along with their food and excreted in the guano. Left undisturbed, the guano accumulates on the floors of the caves, forming discrete animal strata. Dr. Petit's theory is that the quantities of environmental poisons in a layer of guano are accurate measures of their concentrations in the area surrounding the cave when the guano was deposited.

Some of the bat colonies, especially the Mexican free tails, have returned yearly to the same cave for three centuries and more. A precise record of pollutants in this relatively near past—too recent for most other techniques to date with sufficient accuracy—would reveal the year-by-year impact of industrialized man on the environment. By the same token, Dr. Petit's research may establish a sensitive technique for establishing realistic standards of pollution control in the future. Dr. Petit explains:

> For example, suppose we find that over the next ten years pollution-control techniques can reduce the level of mercury at Carlsbad Caverns by a factor of ten. This may be meaningless if we learn from analysis of guano in the caverns that the level existing there 300 years ago was down by a factor of 10,000. If, on the other hand, we find that ambient levels in the area today are no greater than they were 300 years ago, the unreasonableness of initiating costly pollution-control measures and setting unrealistic standards for that area will be apparent.

Pursuing the bats to their inner sanctums demands both ingenuity and stamina. To locate likely caves, Petit collects

lore from local old-timers, hunters, and gas-station attendants, as well as from fellow scientists. He also has been able to enlist the bats themselves in revealing their hideaways. During all-night vigils he snares thirsty bats in a gossamer "mist net," stretched like a tennis net over likely watering places. To his tiny captives he attaches even tinier radio transmitters of his own devising, powered by hearing-aid batteries. Just before dawn on successive nights, he releases the "bugged" bats from two different locations. If he has netted members of the same colony, Petit can track their signals as they wing homeward and thereby triangulate the approximate spot where they disappear into their cave.

But tracking bats is easier on maps than over the rugged relief of the southwestern mountains. One early morning last May, under an Iberian sky of bottomless blue, Petit forsook a comfortable Tucson motel to search for a cave hidden somewhere along a remote, rocky ridge in the Patagonia range. During two days of painstaking mountaineering around the highest rock outcroppings the previous fall, Petit had failed to find it.

This time, the search covered the slightly lower altitudes, just below the three peaks that punctuated the ridgeline. The two-rut road ended far below; Petit had to make the climb on foot. Near the top of a meadow so steep that the ascent required a series of traverses, his tiring pace quickened, refreshed by a breeze perfumed with guano coming from a fissure no more than six inches high at the back of a shallow rock overhang. After a short scramble uphill around the base of the peak, Petit found the cave's front door, a man-high portal invisible from above and below.

Petit also found disheartening evidence that he was not the first visitor to the cave: The floor was littered with the debris of modern trespassers—tin cans and odds and ends of plastic. Clearly the disturbed guano on the floor would be useless for dating, which depends on strict stratification of annual deposits. Searching the dark recesses of the main chamber, however, Petit discovered a narrow chimney leading to a second story. Exploring cautiously, careful not to disturb the deep carpet of guano, he made his way into the upper room. The narrow beam from his headlamp divided the utter darkness. As Petit's gaze swept the room, the light revealed, stroke by stroke, a world apart—a bat's sanctuary locked in the fastness of the rock. This upper chamber showed no sign of previous human intruders.

The same expedition included a return visit to a cave in Eagle Creek Canyon, in the Gila mountain range. The cave was especially valuable for validating Petit's techniques, because it had been literally vacuum-cleaned of its guano deposits for commercial fertilizer in 1954. Thus, its present layers of guano could be dated with certainty from that year. Moreover, the operation of a massive copper mine and smelter nearby provided a clear test of Petit's hypothesis that the guano would reveal changes through time in the concentrations of industrial effluents in the environment.

Inside the cave the sibilant voice of Eagle Creek gave way to the caterwauling of Mexican free-tailed bats, the vanguard of the summer population. They huddled head down, shoulder-to-shoulder on the ceiling, dropping off in squadrons to fly swift, tight formations in the gloom. Petit estimated three hundred thousand of them, darting through the upturned beam of his light like warplanes on a night raid, miraculously avoiding certain suicide against the cave walls. Later in the season, he knew, the population might explode to several million, feeding on local insects by night, breeding, dying. On the wing inside the huge cavern, they would crowd the air, colliding with intruders and each other despite their sensitive sonar. Their droppings would saturate the top layer of guano on the floor, and the smell of concentrated ammonia would make the cave inhospitable to visiting scientists. Now, however, early in the season, they had plenty of airspace for their maneuvers, and their droppings floated down like the gentlest rain. Petit's baseball cap was protection enough from above, and the smell from underfoot was no worse than the bouquet of common garden fertilizer.

Dr. Petit's scientific guano-sampling kit consists of nothing more than a length of common stovepipe, which he drives down into the deposit with any handy rock. He then shovels the surrounding guano away so that the

stovepipe can be sealed with wax, top and bottom, for the journey back to the Fort Collins laboratory. There the sample is impregnated with paraffin to prevent crumbling before the stovepipe is slit open lengthwise, laying bare the strata for consecutive dating. A sample of the guano from each layer is subjected to sophisticated testing procedures for measuring its burden of environmental poisons.

His test results so far lend support to Dr. Petit's hypothesis. Analysis of the guano samples from Eagle Creek Canyon shows evidence of the mercury wastes associated with the nearby copper industry, correlating closely with fluctuations in the smelter's activity. The correlation is so sensitive that Dr. Petit's graph of the mercury content in his guano samples dips sharply to correspond to the two years when strikes crippled the smelter.

If Dr. Petit can carry his measurements far enough into the past—into guano deposited before man's industrial by-products were added to the environment—his technique will offer a standard for measuring the impact of industry on the environment and on ourselves.

Starting Time		Finishing Time	
Reading Time		Reading Rate	
Comprehension		Vocabulary	

Comprehension— Read the following questions and statements. For each one, put an *x* in the box before the option that contains the most complete or accurate answer. Check your answers in the Answer Key on page 107.

1. Dr. Petit tracks down bat caves by
   □ a. putting radio transmitters on bats.
   □ b. following trails of bat guano.
   □ c. analyzing maps of local terrain.
   □ d. observing the flight patterns of bats.

2. The droppings of bats
   □ a. reflect man's effect on the environment.
   □ b. pollute natural scenic wonders.
   □ c. interfere with nature's delicate balance.
   □ d. interfere with scientific investigation.

3. Dr. Petit found the Patagonia cave useful only because
   □ a. previous visitors had not disturbed any bat guano in the main chamber.
   □ b. no human intruders had entered the cave's second story.
   □ c. it was located near a copper mine.
   □ d. he reached it during the bat's mating season.

4. Dr. Petit can draw significant conclusions from his research by using which of the following techniques?
   □ a. carbon dating
   □ b. photosynthesis
   □ c. comparative analysis
   □ d. radiobiology

5. The technique used by Dr. Petit is useful in dealing with the
   - ☐ a. recent past.
   - ☐ b. bat population.
   - ☐ c. prehistoric past.
   - ☐ d. daily guano accumulation.

6. Dr. Petit's theory seems to be
   - ☐ a. confusing to the untrained person.
   - ☐ b. unlikely, considering the habits of bats.
   - ☐ c. resented by business and industry.
   - ☐ d. based on reasonable assumptions.

7. Dr. Petit's cave explorations suggest that bats are
   - ☐ a. dangerous.
   - ☐ b. supernatural.
   - ☐ c. harmless.
   - ☐ d. destructive.

8. The tone of this selection is
   - ☐ a. gloomy.
   - ☐ b. scornful.
   - ☐ c. serious.
   - ☐ d. amused.

9. Dr. Petit seems to be a
   - ☐ a. resented meddler.
   - ☐ b. popular teacher.
   - ☐ c. thorough investigator.
   - ☐ d. misunderstood scientist.

10. The description of bats "darting through the upturned beam of [Dr. Petit's] light like war planes on a night raid . . ." is an example of
   - ☐ a. a simile.
   - ☐ b. a metaphor.
   - ☐ c. an overstatement.
   - ☐ d. an allusion.

Comprehension Skills

1. recalling specific facts	6. making a judgment
2. retaining concepts	7. making an inference
3. organizing facts	8. recognizing tone
4. understanding the main idea	9. understanding characters
5. drawing a conclusion	10. appreciation of literary forms

Study Skills, Part One—Following is a passage with blanks where words have been omitted. Next to the passage are groups of five words, one group for each blank. Complete the passage by selecting the correct word for each of the blanks.

The Art of Writing, III

The first four steps taken by a student in organizing his writing are: (1) state a subject, (2) limit the subject, (3) clarify the purpose, and (4) support the ideas. The next steps are the following.

DISTINGUISH FACT FROM OPINION

In every essay or theme, the writer presents both facts and opinions regarding the subject. A student whose writing approach is ___(1)___ frequently fails to identify for the reader which of his ideas are facts and which are opinions. As one would expect, this leaves the reader hanging and ___(2)___ —uncertain as to the validity of the writer's conclusions.

Present the facts clearly for your reader to see and understand. Then state opinions based on those facts for the reader to appraise and ___(3)___ . The reader can decide intelligently to agree or disagree with you. This is an instance of effective ___(4)___ at work.

STRUCTURE THE PRESENTATION

A writer's organization must be clear to the reader; the reader must be able to see how a theme or essay is

(1)   disorganized   prepared
       forceful   organized   concise

(2)   content   confused
       unprepared   unfulfilled   satisfied

(3)   eradicate   emancipate
       evaluate   accept   amend

(4)   retaliation   communication
       concentration   isolation   stimulation

structured. Unstructured writing is disorganized—the reader does not know where you are leading him and he is unable to see the logic of your discussion. The reader needs to be aware of the ___(5)___ in a subject—when one aspect of a discussion is completed and another is introduced. The reader also needs to be aware of the ___(6)___ made in the presentation of a case. Only then can the reader put the pieces together intelligently.

JUSTIFY THE CONCLUSION

A sign of the inexperienced writer is a statement of conclusion that is not ___(7)___ or supported by the evidence. To the writer, a conclusion may be obvious because of his research into the subject. The reader, however, cannot be expected to "buy" a conclusion unless all the facts supporting it are given.

(5)   purpose   additions   divisions   theme   attitude

(6)   advances   accusations   discoveries   references   transitions

(7)   equal   obvious   justified   approved   enjoyed

Study Skills, Part Two—Read the study skills passage again, paying special attention to the lesson being taught. Then, without looking back at the passage, complete each sentence below by writing in the missing word or words. Check the Answer Key on page 107 for the answers to Study Skills, Part One, and Study Skills, Part Two.

1. A writer presents both facts and opinions about the _____ .

2. A disorganized writer fails to _____ the ideas that are facts and those that are opinions.

3. After the facts and opinions have been presented, the reader must decide whether or not to _____ with the writer.

4. If the writer is organized, he is able to lead the reader and show him the _____ of the discussion.

5. A writer's conclusions must be supported by the _____ .

8 New Use for Old Cars

by Anthony Wolff

Vocabulary—The five words below are from the story you are about to read. Study the words and their meanings. Then complete the ten sentences that follow, using one of the five words to fill in the blank in each sentence. Mark your answer by writing the letter of the word on the line before the sentence. Check your answers in the Answer Key on page 107.

A. derelict: abandoned

B. vintage: old, but of high quality

C. prowess: superior skill or ability

D. corollary: an idea resulting from a previous idea

E. finite: having bounds; limited

_____ 1. Dr. Monroe Wechsler hopes to salvage many of America's old _____ cars.

_____ 2. There is a _____ amount of ore on this earth.

_____ 3. Frederick Schmidt has shown great _____ in solving the problem of auto scrap.

_____ 4. The streets of New York City have become a graveyard for _____ automobiles.

_____ 5. The Environmental Protection Agency tries to spend its _____ resources wisely.

_____ 6. Belief in the value of recycling auto scrap is a _____ to the belief that waste is destructive.

_____ 7. Cars which are particularly well built may someday become _____ models.

_____ 8. Not all researchers have demonstrated the _____ that Dr. Wechsler's team has shown.

_____ 9. Big Steel's opposition to the Ames auto-scrap project is a _____ to the steel industry's heavy investment in ore mills.

_____ 10. Dr. Wechsler's car is considered a _____ model.

A defunct automobile, like a used paper towel or an empty pop bottle, is a disposable item in America. To the car's final owner, junking his old car may be a matter of less concern than finding an overnight parking place for his new one. But for a small group of metallurgists working under Dr. Monroe S. Wechsler at the University of Iowa in Ames, this year's junk could be the potential raw material for next year's model, and the derelict auto junkyard a rich lode of high-assay ore. Though Dr. Wechsler himself drives—gently—a vintage Volvo that shows no signs of decrepitude, he and his colleagues are out to rescue the cars that are rusting away on the scrap heap and recycle them into shiny new steel.

What Dr. Wechsler and his team are looking for is a metallurgical solution to an economic foul-up. Fifteen percent of the six to eight million cars junked in the United States each year are never reprocessed. They remain stalled forever in the junkyards, adding a million more useless hulks to an inventory that already totals 15 to 20 million. Weighing an average 1,400 pounds each, these car corpses represent hundreds of million of tons of ore laboriously torn from the earth, 10 to 14 million tons of metal exactingly processed and manufactured, and billions of dollars spent—all come to an economic dead-end. There is so little demand for auto scrap that an estimated 12 percent of all cars never even make it to the junkyard. Recently, over 80,000 of them were simply abandoned on the streets of New York City alone in one year, not worth the cost of towing. Untotaled thousands more mar the countryside across America.

Analyzing this junkyard traffic jam, the Ames researchers found there is a bottleneck between the auto wrecker, who strips the corpse of its radio, radiator, and other salable parts, and the auto-scrap dealer, who buys the remaining steel carcass from him and processes it for resale. One major obstacle to this flow is that the wrecker cannot extract all the nonferrous "contaminants"—especially copper, but also nickel, aluminum, and chromium—that are part of the auto body.

The steel industry has a limited appetite for contaminated scrap: as little as 0.3 percent copper, for instance—just four pounds in a 1,400-pound auto hulk—may cause imperfections in their new product. So the scrap dealer can't buy all the auto wrecker's dead bodies, and they pile up in roadside junkyards where they offend beauty-lovers and metallurgists alike.

As a professional soldier might measure a nation by its military strength, or a poet by its literary prowess, so Frederick Schmidt, the principal investigator on the auto-scrap project at Ames and a twenty-year veteran

Innovative approaches to auto recycling offer a means for conserving important nonrenewable resources.

metallurgist, believes with a mixture of faith and reason that "a country's strength depends on its ability to handle metals." From that creed, it is only a short logical jump to the corollary that a nation that squanders metal dissipates its strength. For Schmidt there's something immoral in that.

In his unglamorous, uncomfortable office, with its tabletops, shelves, and boxes crowded with bottled samples of his precious pure metals, Schmidt can chalktalk a layman through the ABC's of auto scrap, and at the same time persuade him that finding a way to recycle the stuff is "a way to do something for our country."

Schmidt has a point. The recycling of junked metal is *not* primarily a matter of aesthetics, but of conserving nonrenewable resources of which steel mills devour terrifying quantities in relation to world supply.

At first, the Ames group concentrated on several ways of melting auto scrap in a vacuum to separate out the impurities. In one vacuum process, a bar of compacted scrap, identical in composition to auto scrap, is bombarded with electrons from a gun very much like the one at the rear of a TV tube, but many times more powerful and focused on a much smaller area. Visible only through a protective filter, the tip of the scrap "compact" glows red, then white, and eventually melts into a water-cooled mold below. In the molten puddle at the top of the mold, some of the heat-excited atoms of metal evaporate into the very thin air of the vacuum; condensing on the walls of the experimental chamber to await later recovery. The electron-beam-melting experiments succeed in removing 90 percent of the copper and tin from the scrap, while evaporating only 8 percent of the iron. The rest hardens in the mold into an almost pure ingot, ready for reuse.

Although they yield promising results, the vacuum melting experiments also reveal some problems. Not the least of them is the vacuum itself, a difficult and expensive condition to maintain on an industrial scale. Also, it has been demonstrated that some significant impurities—chromium and nickel, for instance—cannot be separated from iron by vacuum melting because the iron evaporates before they do.

With their initial study already funded by the Environmental Protection Agency and under way, the Ames researchers' interest was drawn to an alternative process that involved neither evaporation nor a vacuum: this innovative line of research, called electroslag remelting, attracted the Rockefeller Foundation's interest. In the electroslag process, electricity flows directly through the scrap "compact" to the mold, passing through a layer of powdered vitreous material—called slag—in between. The slag's high resistance to electricity causes it to heat up, just like the heating element of an electric range. The slag melts; as its temperature rises it in turn melts the bar of scrap. "It's like lowering a wax candle into boiling water," says Schmidt. The slag is concocted with substances that combine readily with the impurities in the scrap: as the molten scrap sinks through the pool of slag, the impurities are filtered out, leaving pure iron.

The trick in the electroslag remelting process is to come up with a slag recipe that includes extractants for all the impurities in the scrap. In theory, according to Schmidt, it should be possible to get them all. The development of the electroslag process is currently proceeding under a new EPA grant, based on the hopeful results of the first year's research. According to the researchers' first-year report, "We believe that electroslag remelting is an extremely promising method for purifying not only auto scrap, but other types of scrap metal such as tin cans, appliances, and selected metal fractions from municipal refuse."

The ultimate proof of the process, of course, will come with its adoption by industry. However, Dr. Wechsler does not anticipate any great enthusiasm from Big Steel for purified auto scrap, no matter how practical and economic the process. He points to the steel industry's huge investment in the "integrated" mills which include ore supplies, transportation, and manufacture, and supply 92 percent of the nation's steel. Indeed, as one observer at Ames comments, "Our biggest enemy has been Big Steel. They pooh-poohed our proposal." Dr. Wechsler foresees that in the beginning his customers for recycled auto scrap are likely to be a growing number of smaller, local "mini-mills." To others, such as the RF's Dr. Ralph Richardson, who recommended the grant-in-aid to the Ames group, all technological innovation starts small, but, says Dr. Richardson, "I can foresee the day when Big Steel, as part of a new plant or in renovating an old one, might give this a try."

"In current terminology," says Dr. Wechsler, "auto scrap has been treated as an economic 'externality.' But as populations grow and the store of resources dwindles in our finite world, such externalities will become of central importance."

Starting Time		Finishing Time	
Reading Time		Reading Rate	
Comprehension		Vocabulary	

Comprehension
— Read the following questions and statements. For each one, put an *x* in the box before the option that contains the most complete or accurate answer. Check your answers in the Answer Key on page 107.

1. If the vacuum melting process were to be used on an industrial scale,
   □ a. the process would have to be supervised.
   □ b. heat-excited atoms would be difficult to control.
   □ c. the enforcement of safety procedures would create a problem.
   □ d. creating and maintaining the vacuum would present a problem.

2. New ways must be found to recycle discarded metal because
   □ a. natural resources are limited.
   □ b. the automobile industry is competitive.
   □ c. the general public is concerned.
   □ d. foreign competition makes it necessary.

3. The Ames group began its research by
   □ a. canvassing auto wreckers to learn why steel from junk cars was not being recycled.
   □ b. perfecting the definition of "junk cars."
   □ c. investigating an electroslag process.
   □ d. developing a vacuum melting process.

4. Doctor Wechsler and his team of metallurgists have devised a way to
   □ a. beautify the countryside.
   □ b. decontaminate metal scrap.
   □ c. prevent metal rust.
   □ d. eliminate auto junkyards.

5. The problem of abandoned cars and eyesore junkyards is really a problem of
   □ a. greed.
   □ b. apathy.
   □ c. economics.
   □ d. organization.

6. The vacuum and electroslag techniques
   □ a. depend heavily upon electrical power.
   □ b. are equally preferred by scientists.
   □ c. create more problems than they solve.
   □ d. are inexpensive to implement.

7. It can be inferred from the selection that
   □ a. Big Steel is interested in conservation.
   □ b. the strength of a nation is measured by its literature.
   □ c. tomorrow's needs must be met today.
   □ d. natural resources will be available to satisfy demands.

8. The tone of the selection is
   □ a. factual.   □ c. conciliatory.
   □ b. argumentative.   □ d. dogmatic.

9. Frederick Schmidt is
   □ a. an organized man.   □ c. a confused scientist.
   □ b. a convincing person. □ d. a boring person.

10. The phrase ". . . the auto wrecker, who strips the corpse of its radio, radiator, and other salable parts . . ." is an example of
    □ a. simile.
    □ b. fallacy.
    □ c. eccentricity.
    □ d. personification.

Comprehension Skills

1. recalling specific facts	6. making a judgment
2. retaining concepts	7. making an inference
3. organizing facts	8. recognizing tone
4. understanding the main idea	9. understanding characters
5. drawing a conclusion	10. appreciation of literary forms

Study Skills, Part One—Following is a passage with blanks where words have been omitted. Next to the passage are groups of five words, one group for each blank. Complete the passage by selecting the correct word for each of the blanks.

How to Use Word Context

During political campaigns in election years, we invariably hear one candidate accuse an opponent of quoting him "out of context." The danger in taking a speaker's ___(1)___ out of context is that a sentence by itself may imply a meaning entirely different from the meaning it had conveyed when surrounded by other thoughts.

This suggests an important aspect of word usage: a word's true meaning depends upon ___(2)___ it is used. This is readily apparent in the case of ambiguous words, like *bow* or *sink*. Context tells the reader when a *bow tied with ribbon* is meant rather than a *bow to the audience*. Similarly, without knowing the ___(3)___ the reader does not know whether the writer is referring to *sink* as in *water* or *sink* as in *kitchen*.

Not so apparent is the effect of context on words generally thought to have ___(4)___ and unchanging meaning. The word *conventional* in one context may suggest all that is stable, reliable, and in the most time-honored tradition. In another context *conventional* could imply staleness, the refusal to change or adapt to modern ways.

Beginning as youngsters, we add to our understanding of a word's ___(5)___ every time we hear it or use it. For example, the first few times you heard the word *school,* you may have understood it to mean a place where older brothers and sisters spend most of the day. Later, *school* came to mean a place where things are learned. Today, your understanding of the word encompasses several comprehensive ideas.

This same growth pattern occurs with other words. As a student, you will come across new words, or words

(1)   life   words
     reputation   friends   thoughts

(2)   how   when
     why   where   how often

(3)   rules   training
     motivation   context   background

(4)   varying   consistent
     continuing   traditional   unimaginative

(5)   history   potential
     meaning   popularity   power

you only vaguely understand. Being aware of the way words function in context helps you to understand these words and make them part of your ___(6)___ . Each time you hear an unfamiliar word, the context it is being used in will add to your understanding. With repeated exposure, you will come to understand all that the word ___(7)___ , and eventually you will be able to use it comfortably in your writing and speaking.

(6)   comprehension   environment
        understanding   education   vocabulary

(7)   denies   imagines
        rejects   implies   overcomes

Study Skills, Part Two—Read the study skills passage again, paying special attention to the lesson being taught. Then, without looking back at the passage, complete each sentence below by writing in the missing word or words. Check the Answer Key on page 107 for the answers to Study Skills, Part One, and Study Skills, Part Two.

1. Quoting a speaker's words out of context may result in conveying an

   _____ meaning.

2. Some words are _____ and change meaning completely when used

   in different contexts.

3. Context may also have an unexpected _____ on words

   generally thought to have unchanging meanings.

4. As we hear words used several times in many ways, a _____

   pattern occurs.

5. Complete understanding of a word results in the ability to use it correctly in

   _____ and in speaking.

9 The Anatomy of Drink, I

by Rog Halegood

Vocabulary—The five words below are from the story you are about to read. Study the words and their meanings. Then complete the ten sentences that follow, using one of the five words to fill in the blank in each sentence. Mark your answer by writing the letter of the word on the line before the sentence. Check your answers in the Answer Key on page 107.

A. deterred: prevented; discouraged

B. fiasco: a complete failure

C. assaying: analyzing

D. scatological: obscene

E. soporific: sleep-inducing

_____ 1. The consumption of alcohol reduces our inhibitions against _____ behavior.

_____ 2. After a person has consumed eight drinks, _____ his or her blood will reveal an alcohol level of about 0.35 percent.

_____ 3. The fact that alcohol can be a killer has not _____ most people from drinking.

_____ 4. Some people drink alcohol for its _____ effects.

_____ 5. A simple blood test is used in _____ a person's level of drunkenness.

_____ 6. Moslems are _____ from consuming alcohol by religious laws.

_____ 7. A person is more apt to engage in _____ acts when drunk than when sober.

_____ 8. The consumption of too much alcohol can turn a pleasant evening into a _____ .

_____ 9. An attempt to ban all alcohol from society is likely to be a _____ .

_____ 10. Alcohol is a _____ drug.

Alcoholism appears to be as old as the history of alcoholic beverages—a history which is ancient indeed. In the *Wisdom of Ani,* an ancient Egyptian book of proverbs and moral codes, warnings are given against the unwise imbibing too much drink. The Bible, too, is dotted with references to the misuse of alcohol; the "drunkenness of Noah"

Used unwisely, alcohol can destroy everything it enhances. It is a terrifying double-edged sword.

is a story known to every school child. The Moslems forbid alcohol all together, and in some countries of that faith the mere possession of it is a capital offense. Yet, stern legislation against alcohol seems never to have deterred the general populace from having its full share. The English were at a loss to stem the phenomenal addiction to gin that ravaged British society during the 18th century; the Volstead Act in the United States was a total fiasco and introduced an element of organized crime which still plagues us. In fact, history has proven that the more a society tries to repress alcohol consumption, the more that consumption is desired and sought after. Plainly, the safe use of alcohol lies in the successful implementation of sensible drinking programs, not wholesale policies of repression and enforced abstinence.

Man likes to drink. The fact is made evident when one considers the incredible list of ingredients that man has fermented and cheerfully ingested: bananas, grapefruit, persimmons, mare's milk, honey, animal blood, rice, all grains, dandelions—the list is endless and limited only by imagination. Thousands of organic substances are capable of fermentation, and man appears to have fermented just about everything, at one time or another, in the search for a "better" potable. Few areas of human endeavor seem to have brought as much ingenuity to bear as some of the ways by which man has arrived at something new to drink; indeed, many men have devoted their entire lives to the pursuit of one new and glorious distillation. Some, like the Catholic abbot Dom Perignon, succeeded brilliantly. (Perignon is credited with the invention of champagne.)

The reason man has devoted such an exorbitant amount of time to such a nonessential pursuit is quite obvious: alcoholic beverages are a pleasure to drink. Alcohol is nature's own tranquilizer—Everyman's Librium. Taken in small quantities, it eases life's many pains and troubles. It provides relaxation and good cheer, a sense of well-being and comradeship. These beneficial properties of alcohol have been realized by man since recorded history, and probably long before that. At the same time, man has realized also that alcohol is a terrifying double-edged sword. Used unwisely, it is capable of destroying everything it enhances: sociability, marriage, livelihood, productivity. It can reduce a man to a state lower than an animal, and

it can kill him ultimately through a hundred deaths. Alcohol *is* a great destroyer, but it need not be such. The fault is not that of alcohol itself, but in the way it is used. All programs of sensible drinking must start with that ultimate fact.

What happens when I drink?

Alcohol is a drug. It acts on the central nervous system as a depressant *(not as a stimulant).* Normally, it first produces euphoria or a feeling of well-being, then a certain amount of sedation interpreted as relaxation, then intoxication, and, finally, death. Each of these stages is governed by the amount and rate of alcohol entering the bloodstream of the drinker. There is no hocus-pocus involved here. The amount of alcohol in the system can be precisely determined at any time by means of a common blood test. However, the degree of effect of alcohol upon any given person is determined by many factors: weight, amount of food in the stomach at the time alcohol is ingested, the emotional outlook of the person at the time he is drinking, previous drinking history, and overall tolerance to the drug. These factors, and others, can alter the absorption rate of alcohol into the system. Still, the level of alcohol in the blood is the final determinant for assaying states through sobriety into full-fledged drunkenness. As the alcohol level rises, specific physiological and psychological changes can be safely predicted.

The formula works this way: one shot of liquor (one and one-half ounces) will place the alcohol concentration in the blood at approximately 0.03 percent, or 0.03 grams of alcohol for every 100 c.c. of blood. These figures are based on an average adult male of about 150 pounds; the concentration would be higher for most women and children, of course. Now, at this level, it is virtually impossible to label anyone as intoxicated. However, the second drink, if taken within an hour of the first, will raise the alcohol in the blood to a little more than 0.05 percent, and we begin to experience alcohol's first plateau: we feel relaxed, more talkative. Our problems don't seem quite as pressing, and the company around us suddenly seems more pleasant, more "fun to be with." We are still not drunk in any legal sense, and our judgment and physical coordination is virtually unimpaired. So far, so good.

Somewhere between the third and fourth drink, things begin to happen rapidly. With the fourth drink, our alcohol concentration has reached 0.10 percent, or more, and we can at last be classified as legally drunk. The people we are with may still be "fun," but we're not noticing them as much as we did earlier. We are really becoming more introspective, although we may be the "life of the party" since our normal inhibitions against outrageous or scatological conduct have been repressed. It is at this point that we make the pass at the cocktail waitress, or guffaw too loudly at a dirty joke. Our brain is reacting to the soporific effects of alcohol, and our motor functions are becoming "loose" and uncoordinated. It is at this level that we are a definite hazard on the highway, and most states now consider a blood-alcohol analysis of 0.10 percent as legal evidence for drunkenness.

But it's New Year's, or Armistice Day, or the boss-just-fired-me day, or the mother-in-law-is-here-to-stay day, so we have a few more. The sixth drink jumps our alcohol level to between 0.15 and 0.20 percent. At this level, we are almost unrecognizable, both to ourselves and others. If sleep doesn't overtake us, we are likely to undergo violent changes in our mood and behavior. We may laugh one minute, cry the next. We may pick a fight, or take our clothes off on Main Street. We are no longer in control of our actions, and our behavior is completely unpredictable. If we drive in this state, we stand a high chance of killing ourselves and others.

But let's really tie one on, okay? It's very easy to do. The only requirement is that we stay awake long enough to keep pouring back the hooch. At about the eighth continuous drink, the alcohol level in our blood will rise to somewhere around 0.35 percent. Most of us can't walk at this level, so we had better just stay at the bar provided we can still get service. Better still, we can check into a hotel with a bottle and there'll be no one to bother us. The company we were with lost their charm a long time ago, and it's better to be by ourselves.

Somewhere between the eleventh and thirteenth drink, our alcohol level jumps to 0.50 percent and we suddenly can't drink another drop. Reason: We have passed out. However, if we drink very quickly, we might be able to down two or three more before the curtain descends. By doing this, we can pretty well assure ourselves that we may hit the alcohol bull's eye with a blood concentration of 0.55 to 0.60 percent. At this point, we will die in an acute alcoholic coma and our little drinking bout comes to a sudden close.

We are talking here of facts, not fiction. While tolerance to alcohol, and other factors, may allow one person to drink more than another, the alcohol concentrations mentioned above will produce the effects exactly as described, plus hundreds of others not mentioned. Alcohol is a drug. It cannot be played with without endangering life itself. It can be consumed *safely*, and that is the whole purpose of sane drinking practices.

I'm drunk. What do I do now?

When you become drunk, the only cure is to stop drinking. Coffee will not sober you up. Steam baths will do nothing. Exercise is of no avail. Only time can bring you back to a sober state.

The body's system must oxidize all the alcohol which is ingested. It does this at a rate of approximately .015 percent an hour. The rule of thumb is to allow about one hour of sobering up time for each drink consumed. It takes this long for alcohol to be eliminated within the system. Beyond the one drink an hour limit, alcohol accumulates in the bloodstream and only time (and the liver) can remove it. There are no short cuts.

There are, however, ways in which the absorption rate can be slowed. The principal method is by food. It is always better to drink with food in the stomach than to drink on an empty stomach. While this will not save you from overindulgence, it will provide some moderate protection against the first couple of drinks. Similarly, sipping a drink over a long period of time will reduce its net effect.

And that's about it. Anything else you may have heard is probably an old wives' tale. If you drink, alcohol will enter your bloodstream. If you continue to drink, it will accumulate in your bloodstream. That's the pure fact, and anything else is myth.

Starting Time		Finishing Time	
Reading Time		Reading Rate	
Comprehension		Vocabulary	

Comprehension— Read the following questions and statements. For each one, put an *x* in the box before the option that contains the most complete or accurate answer. Check your answers in the Answer Key on page 107.

1. The motivation behind man's production of alcoholic beverages is
   ☐ a. evil.
   ☐ b. humanitarian.
   ☐ c. financial.
   ☐ d. pleasure.

2. The logical progression of uncontrolled alcoholic intake
   ☐ a. will produce a feeling of well-being.
   ☐ b. can result in death.
   ☐ c. can encourage complete relaxation.
   ☐ d. will result in drunkenness.

3. The first noticeable effects of alcohol consumption are
   - ☐ a. relaxation and a boost in spirits.
   - ☐ b. sleepiness.
   - ☐ c. loss of coordination.
   - ☐ d. violent mood changes.

4. Which of the following best expresses the main idea of the selection?
   - ☐ a. Never drink on an empty stomach.
   - ☐ b. If you drink, don't drive.
   - ☐ c. Social drinking leads to alcoholism.
   - ☐ d. Alcohol should be used, not abused.

5. The proper use of alcohol requires
   - ☐ a. social acceptance.
   - ☐ b. self-restraint.
   - ☐ c. financial independence.
   - ☐ d. congenial company.

6. The search for the ultimate drink has produced
   - ☐ a. trash as well as excellence.
   - ☐ b. temperance along with enjoyment.
   - ☐ c. quality and high prices.
   - ☐ d. confusion and rivalry.

7. As the alcohol level rises in the bloodstream, its effects
   - ☐ a. level off gradually.
   - ☐ b. baffle medical science.
   - ☐ c. heighten mental awareness.
   - ☐ d. can be predicted mathematically.

8. The author's tone can best be described as
   - ☐ a. sarcastic.
   - ☐ b. emotional.
   - ☐ c. blunt.
   - ☐ d. moralistic.

9. The author seems motivated by a desire to
   - ☐ a. panic his readers.
   - ☐ b. encourage his readers.
   - ☐ c. help people use alcohol wisely.
   - ☐ d. stop everyone from drinking alcohol.

10. The statement that alcohol can kill a man "through a hundred deaths"
   - ☐ a. is an exaggeration.
   - ☐ b. alludes to the many different forms an alcohol-related death can take.
   - ☐ c. means it takes many alcoholic binges before death can result.
   - ☐ d. refers to the many different types of alcohol that can be fatal.

Comprehension Skills

1. recalling specific facts	6. making a judgment
2. retaining concepts	7. making an inference
3. organizing facts	8. recognizing tone
4. understanding the main idea	9. understanding characters
5. drawing a conclusion	10. appreciation of literary forms

Study Skills, Part One—Following is a passage with blanks where words have been omitted. Next to the passage are groups of five words, one group for each blank. Complete the passage by selecting the correct word for each of the blanks.

Contextual Aids, I

Context helps us in a way no dictionary can. Various shades and richness of meaning cannot be gained from dictionary definitions alone; we must see the word used to grasp its ___(1)___ meaning.

Studies of good readers show that they are ___(2)___ of the different contexts in which words are set. These are commonly referred to as contextual aids. Using contextual aids intelligently is the reader's most important vocabulary tool. And it is a reading skill which can be mastered and developed.

1. Common Expressions. Words can be recognized as part of a common phrase or idiomatic expression. Certain phrases and expressions are used ___(3)___ and become well known to the reader. A word omitted can readily be supplied because of its familiarity.

(1)		new	foreign
	full	predicted	opposite
(2)		oblivious	forgetful
	suspicious	aware	fond
(3)		regularly	always
	rarely	sometimes	correctly

In the old saying *His bark is worse than his* _____ , the reader can easily fill in the missing word, *bite*. If you came across this expression in your reading, you could ___(4)___ supply any missing elements of this familiar saying.

2. Modifying Phrases. Words can be understood and recognized through the use of phrases which modify the ___(5)___ word. Frequently a word is accompanied by a prepositional phrase which modifies it, giving the reader valuable ___(6)___ to understanding and recognition. For example, if you were to read the sentence _____ *by the finest artists of our century were displayed at the exhibit,* you could easily ___(7)___ that the missing word is *paintings.* The phrase *by the finest artists* is the contextual aid which acts as the clue.

(4)   never   occasionally
painfully   automatically   probably

(5)   implied   spoken
familiar   unknown   written

(6)   decisions   judgments
clues   choices   deterrents

(7)   learn   guess
hope   deny   imply

Study Skills, Part Two—Read the study skills passage again, paying special attention to the lesson being taught. Then, without looking back at the passage, complete each sentence below by writing in the missing word or words. Check the Answer Key on page 107 for the answers to Study Skills, Part One, and Study Skills, Part Two.

1. Dictionary definitions are not the only source of _____ .

2. Using contextual aids is an important reading _____ .

3. Words that are a part of a _____ phrase are easily recognized.

4. The word omitted can be supplied because of its _____ .

5. Unknown words can sometimes be understood through the use of accompanying phrases which _____ the words.

10 | **The Anatomy of Drink, II**

by Rog Halegood

Vocabulary—The five words below are from the story you are about to read. Study the words and their meanings. Then complete the ten sentences that follow, using one of the five words to fill in the blank in each sentence. Mark your answer by writing the letter of the word on the line before the sentence. Check your answers in the Answer Key on page 107.

A. premise: a fact or belief on which another belief is based

B. ingestion: intake

C. insidious: treacherous; appealing but harmful

D. delude: deceive

E. predispose: make susceptible to; incline toward in advance

_____ 1. Alcoholism is an _____ and sometimes deadly disease.

_____ 2. A person's life-style or habits may _____ him or her to alcoholism.

_____ 3. Beer drinkers often _____ themselves into thinking their drinking habits are perfectly safe.

_____ 4. Daily _____ of alcohol does not necessarily equal alcoholism.

_____ 5. Many victims of alcoholism have a hard time admitting they suffer from this _____ disease.

_____ 6. We should not _____ ourselves with the notion that alcoholics are skid row bums.

_____ 7. Most doctors now act on the _____ that alcoholism is an addictive illness.

_____ 8. People with patterns of frequent drinking should note that such patterns may _____ them to alcoholism.

_____ 9. People use many rationalizations for their _____ of alcohol.

_____ 10. Alcoholics often operate on the mistaken _____ that they can stop drinking whenever they choose.

Alcoholism is a disease that cannot be cured, only arrested.

Every year, doctors treat patients for alcoholism who swear that they can't be alcoholics. They base this belief on the premise that all they've ever drunk in their lives is beer. So they have one or two six-packs a day, so what? Beer, after all, has almost "no alcohol." On first glance, it seems a pretty logical argument. Beer does contain only four percent alcohol. But the alcohol is by volume, and therein lies the rub. An ounce of beer contains four percent alcohol. An ounce of 86 proof whiskey contains 43 percent alcohol. While many people stop drinking after one ounce of whiskey, who has ever drunk just one ounce of beer? You drink 10 ounces, or 20 ounces, and you have increased your alcohol ingestion in direct proportion to the alcohol content by *volume*. Therefore, one average mug-and-a-half of beer equals, in alcohol content, about that of one drink. Likewise, a normal sized glass of wine equals one beer, or approximately one drink.

The effects of wine and beer are slightly less noticeable because the alcohol is more diluted by volume than in straight spirits. Similarly, one can retard the effects of hard liquor by mixing it with water or a commercial mixer. On the other hand, about the fastest-acting popular cocktail is the straight-up martini, either of the gin or vodka variety. The proof is high, and the drink unadulterated; consequently, robbed of any "buffering" agent such as water, the alcohol from such a drink enters the bloodstream very quickly. Few are the men, boasts to the contrary, who can imbibe two martinis at lunch and have their work for the rest of the day unimpaired. It would be impossible to calculate the number of man-hours lost every week in the United States as a direct result of the martini luncheon.

Who drinks, and why?

Ninety-five million Americans drink something alcoholic at least once a year; that leaves about 32 percent of the adult United States populace as absolute teetotalers. Of the ninety-five million drinkers, at least nine million develop serious alcohol-related problems. But, the most startling fact of all, the nine million problem drinkers affect the lives of more than 36 million people! This is the awful legacy of the problem drinker. If his drinking harmed only himself, his problem would not fall too heavily upon the shoulders of society. But when 36 million people are involved as a result of his problem, the situation becomes an urgent one.

The fact is that heavy drinking kills—and not just the drinker. Fully half of all highway fatalities are alcohol-related. This means that on the average more than 28,000 people lose their lives on the United States highway system a year as a partial contribution to alcohol misuse. This fact alone is enough to rivet us all into a position of taking a serious look at alcohol in the daily pattern of our social fabric.

But the statistics don't end on the highway. Fully one-third of all homicides in our country are also alcohol-related. And arrests where alcohol is a factor average close to two million a year.

In dollars, something we are fond of considering, alcohol costs industry, and the American worker and taxpayer, more than $15 billion annually in medical expenses, lost time, accidents, and impaired job efficiency.

On the other side of the coin, Americans spend more than $20 billion each year on alcoholic beverages. The federal government spends less than $4 million a year on alcohol research and alcohol facilities.

Grim as these statistics are, they do not mean that alcohol should once again be prohibited. Clearly, the majority of United States drinkers drink in a sane and safe way. What the figures do prove is that urgent work is needed on the gigantic problem of alcoholism. Nine million lives are directly at stake, plus millions of others who suffer, in one form or another, from the consequences of the alcoholic's problem.

Virtually all medical groups, including the AMA, now recognize alcoholism as an illness. So do many insurance companies and health groups.

We must first instruct the general public in ways of safe drinking, then we must reach the alcoholic himself. Prevention of alcoholism is the first and most important step. This prevention can come about only when all are made aware of the problem. After this, treatment of the alcoholic becomes a much simpler process.

I drink. Am I an alcoholic?

One of the most insidious aspects of the disease of alcoholism is its ability to completely mask itself. Few alcoholics, while in the grips of alcoholism, can admit to themselves that they are diseased. Since no one opens their mouths and physically pours drinks down them, they can always delude themselves that they are in control; i.e. to drink they must make the conscious decision to put glass or bottle in hand, and then to raise that hand to their lips. Since this action is seemingly a voluntary one, alcoholics are provided with the comforting notion that they are operating under their own steam. They can stop drinking any time by closing their fists and their mouths. Nothing could be further from the truth. Alcoholism, regardless of what form it may take, is a physical and/or psychological addiction, and the alcoholic is no more capable of altering his disease than a heroin addict is capable of taking one fix for the day. The disease itself demands alcohol, and an alcoholic cannot be written off as a person with poor willpower. Willpower has nothing to do with the disease itself, although willpower has a lot to do with treatment. There is a very subtle, but very vital difference contained in the last statement. We do not tell cancer patients to cure their disease through willpower, and alcoholism cannot be cured by that approach. Cancer and alcoholism are diseases. Both are treatable, although alcoholism cannot be cured, only arrested.

So, who is the safe drinker? And the question can be a difficult one to answer. Simplistically speaking, the safe drinker is one within whom no rationalization, regardless of how subtle, is necessary for the taking of a drink. Whenever rationalization for drinking comes into play, the danger signal should go up.

If you have a drink because you are offered a drink, and think nothing more beyond that, it's probably quite all right for you to have that drink. If you attend a cocktail party and have one or two drinks, that's probably all right too. *But* if you habitually desire a drink before one is offered, or if you attend that cocktail party solely because you want to drink, then these are potential danger signals. Preoccupation with alcohol—planning when you will drink, what you will drink—are sure signs that alcohol may be playing too large a part in your life. Here again is where the rationalizations become so simple. It is so easy to say, "I'll just have these drinks to be sociable," or, "Of course I want a drink. I've had such a lousy day." The safe drinker is one who does not drink because an excuse is handy. He drinks. Or he doesn't drink. And he doesn't think of the why and wherefores. He takes it, or he leaves it—and one situation is as easy for him to do as the other. Alcohol makes absolutely no difference in his life.

Alcoholism is difficult to define because there are so many types of the disease. It is impossible to give hard-and-fast rules that say this is alcoholism, and this is not. Even the person who drinks daily will not necessarily become an alcoholic, although such a pattern would certainly predispose one to the disease.

Most medical authorities now agree that it is not necessarily how much one drinks that may lead to alcoholism, but *why* one drinks. And this goes right back to the fact of rationalizing drinking behavior. If you must think about booze, then you should probably give it up. If you crave a drink, you should give it up. If drink is more important than food, stop now and seek help. If alcohol in any way alters your life or work, you're facing trouble. If a lunch without a drink sounds dull, booze has become too much a part of your life. All these things, and many more, are urgent red flags on the road to alcoholism; only the foolhardy—or the alcoholic—will fail to notice them.

If you drink frequently to relieve problems, soothe tensions, forget cares, get happy, have a fight, go to bed, calm your stomach, increase your sex life, take a trip, meet people—you are drinking for wrong reasons. Drink for the wrong reasons long enough, and you will have a real reason to drink—alcoholism. Nine million Americans are all drinking for the wrong reasons.

Think all alcoholics are skid row bums? Not so. Less than three percent of all United States derelicts have drinking problems. Today's alcoholic individual is likely to be bright, well-educated, middle or top management, 35 to 50 years of age, a family man, and well-respected in his community and profession. He simply drinks too much, for all the wrong reasons, and his drinking has led to alcoholism.

Starting Time		*Finishing Time*	
Reading Time		*Reading Rate*	
Comprehension		*Vocabulary*	

Comprehension— Read the following questions and statements. For each one, put an *x* in the box before the option that contains the most complete or accurate answer. Check your answers in the Answer Key on page 107.

1. Approximately 36 million Americans
   □ a. are injured in alcohol-related accidents each year.
   □ b. are alcoholics.
   □ c. find their lives affected by alcoholism.
   □ d. are arrested on alcohol-related charges each year.

2. Medical authorities are mainly concerned with
   □ a. the quantity of alcohol people take.
   □ b. the families of alcoholics.
   □ c. legal problems resulting from alcoholism.
   □ d. the reasons which prompt people to drink.

3. A warning sign for drinkers is
   □ a. acceptance of a drink when one is offered.
   □ b. planning when or where to drink.
   □ c. indulging in two martinis over lunch.
   □ d. preferring hard liquor to beer or wine.

4. Considered from the author's point of view, alcohol is a
   □ a. profitable industry.   □ c. rare pleasure.
   □ b. necessary evil.   □ d. costly commodity.

5. The martini luncheon is a
   - ☐ a. boon to the business executive.
   - ☐ b. tradition among retired businessmen.
   - ☐ c. proven obstacle to serious work.
   - ☐ d. legitimate business deduction.

6. The problem drinker is
   - ☐ a. a threat to society.
   - ☐ b. his own best counsel.
   - ☐ c. a misunderstood person.
   - ☐ d. a victim of circumstances.

7. An alcoholic
   - ☐ a. must be willing to receive treatment.
   - ☐ b. has no willpower.
   - ☐ c. can undergo a complete cure.
   - ☐ d. can never hope to control his drinking.

8. The tone of the selection is
   - ☐ a. sober.
   - ☐ b. snide.
   - ☐ c. unkind.
   - ☐ d. encouraging.

9. The unreformed alcoholic is
   - ☐ a. callous and defiant.
   - ☐ b. dishonest with himself and with others.
   - ☐ c. weak and self-indulgent.
   - ☐ d. excitable and full of energy.

10. The phrase "under their own steam" means
   - ☐ a. in an alcoholic daze.
   - ☐ b. while they are still angry.
   - ☐ c. without outside help or interference.
   - ☐ d. in control of their environment.

Comprehension Skills

1. recalling specific facts
2. retaining concepts
3. organizing facts
4. understanding the main idea
5. drawing a conclusion
6. making a judgment
7. making an inference
8. recognizing tone
9. understanding characters
10. appreciation of literary forms

Study Skills, Part One—Following is a passage with blanks where words have been omitted. Next to the passage are groups of five words, one group for each blank. Complete the passage by selecting the correct word for each of the blanks.

Contextual Aids, II

3. Accompanying Description. An unknown word can often be understood because it has been ___(1)___ or described in the context. This kind of contextual aid, naturally enough, is commonly used in textbooks. Authors frequently provide a description or definition to ___(2)___ their readers. In the sentence *Students should use _____; these are books containing definitions of words,* the reader would know that the missing word is *dictionaries* because of the accompanying description.

4. Parts of a Series. Whenever items appear in a list or series, the items themselves give clues to the reader. If one of them were omitted from the list, the reader could probably supply it. This is possible because the parts of a series are ___(3)___; they share some feature in common. An additional clue is provided by the connector *and;* this tells the reader that the items are alike in some way. For example, if you see the sentence *The theater was packed with men, women, and _____,* you can confidently fill in the blank with the missing word, *children,* the next word in the series. Notice how the *and* in the series leads you to ___(4)___ another related item.

5. Comparison and Contrast. Unknown or unfamiliar words become ___(5)___ when compared or contrasted with known words. We know that when parallels are being

(1)	found	defined
	emphasized used	denounced

(2)	deter	motivate
	assist reward	hinder

(3)	continuous	compatible
	related foreign	familiar

(4)	expect	know
	reject learn	recognize

(5)	expected	easy
	meaningful difficult	irritating

drawn, like things are being ___(6)___ . In the case of contrast, we are dealing with things that are opposite. The reader's ability to recognize that a comparison or contrast is being made permits him to exploit this type of contextual aid. Take this sentence: *The two brothers were as different as day and _ _ _ _ _ .* It is simple for the reader to complete the ___(7)___ with the word *night.*

(6)	discovered		created
	discarded	examined	related

(7)		contract	series
	classification	comparison	prediction

Study Skills, Part Two—Read the study skills passage again, paying special attention to the lesson being taught. Then, without looking back at the passage, complete each sentence below by writing in the missing word or words. Check the Answer Key on page 107 for the answers to Study Skills, Part One, and Study Skills, Part Two.

1. The definition of words as a contextual aid is often used in _____ .

2. In a list or series, the _____ give clues to the reader.

3. Parts of a series _____ a feature in common.

4. The connector word *and* indicates that items are _____ in some way.

5. In using the contextual aid of contrast, we are dealing with things that are _____ .

11 Textbooks and the Invisible Woman

by Janice Law Trecker

Vocabulary—The five words below are from the story you are about to read. Study the words and their meanings. Then complete the ten sentences that follow, using one of the five words to fill in the blank in each sentence. Mark your answer by writing the letter of the word on the line before the sentence. Check your answers in the Answer Key on page 107.

A. paucity: scarcity

B. manifold: numerous

C. subsidized: gave financial assistance to

D. marshalled: organized

E. purveying: furnishing; providing

_____ 1. Too many history textbooks are guilty of _____ stereotypes about women.

_____ 2. There are _____ examples of history texts ignoring the contributions of women.

_____ 3. Many textbooks suffer from a _____ of appropriate female role models.

_____ 4. Women have not _____ their resources to bring about a change in history textbooks.

_____ 5. The forced labor of male and female slaves _____ Southern farmers.

_____ 6. In most history textbooks there is a distinct _____ of accurate information about women.

_____ 7. Textbooks should not be _____ images of women as weak, subservient, and economically irrelevent to American history.

_____ 8. In the 20th century, more and more women have _____ their families' high standard of living by getting jobs outside the home.

_____ 9. Early American women used a few raw materials to produce _____ goods.

_____ 10. Many examples could be _____ to illustrate the importance of women in the development of American society.

The treatment of women in history textbooks reflects long-held ideas of female inferiority.

Within the last decade and a half, there has been an increasing interest in women's history and women's studies on the college and university level. The resulting new scholarship and material have, however, barely penetrated the secondary level. Despite such promising developments as new supplementary texts on women's history, new resource and audiovisual materials, and a growing concern about the quality of education for women and girls, the amount of women's history taught on the secondary level remains extremely small.

American history textbooks reflect a mythic rather than an historical view of women. Their basic assumption is that history is masculine, and their characteristic belief that society, culture, politics, art, science, and economics are all male domains leads to the wholesale omission of women and to the distortion and minimization of those females who do appear. The clearest evidence for this viewpoint is the fact that 51 percent of the population is usually "covered" by about one page of text.

Of course, the typical textbook is not totally devoid of women's names. There are always a few women too important or too unique to be completely excluded. Harriet Beecher Stowe, Harriet Tubman, Sacajawea, Phillis Wheatley, Clara Barton, Dorothea Dix, and Susan B. Anthony are among the small and exclusive circle of women who are found deserving of a sentence or two.

While there has been a recent noticeable shift to include some history of minorities, the pattern of excluding minority women is evident and what is presented is still a male-only view. Women like Sojourner Truth, the founders of Black educational institutions like Lucy Laney and Mary Bethune, and Fannie Lou Hamer, a founder of the Mississippi Freedom Democratic Party, are never included. Pocahontas is almost always noted (after all, she saved a white male), but the vital and complex role the Clan Mothers in the Hou-den-no-shaun-nee (People of the Longhouse), or as the French called it, the Iroquois Confederacy, is rarely mentioned. Gertrudis Bocanegra, "the Joan of Arc of Mexico," and Mariana Bracetti, the Puerto Rican leader in the El Grito de Lares revolutionary movement—who usually is credited only for sewing its first flag—are invisible heroines in our texts marred by sexism and racism. Lola Rodriguez de Tió, the nineteenth-century feminist, and Juana Colon, the twentieth-century union organizer of women laborers, are but a few examples of the serious omissions that continue to scar our history textbooks.

Their presence, however, only points up the deficiencies in the overall conception of women's place in history. A few "great names" accompanied by a factual statement—without explanation or any analysis—would never qualify as a proper historical treatment for any but "women's issues."

Tokenism is the rule

Tokenism is the rule in the texts' treatment of women, because only females who distinguish themselves in a masculine hierarchy are considered bona fide historical characters. Women who act outside the normal male channels of power—or most of the significant women in America before the twentieth century—are automatically suspect. If they are controversial, they are simply ignored along with whatever cause they may have championed, as are women like Margaret Sanger, Emma Goldman, Ida B. Wells, Mother Jones, Alice Paul, and Rosa Parks.

If, however, it appears to masculine sensibilities that a woman was simply eccentric, she is sure to be included. Providing comic relief is the function of at least half of all so-called women's history in these books. The need for a few light touches insures that hatchet-wielding Carry Nation will be preferred to the brilliant and influential organizer Frances Willard in discussing temperance, and that the Gibson Girl and the Flapper will displace the social reformer or feminist in tracing the evolution of the modern woman. By and large, authors prefer to write sparkling discussions of skirt lengths and hairstyles rather than to dig into such serious topics as the exploitation of female labor, the treatment of women in slavery, or women's role in mass education. A little wit, so conspicuously absent in the other 99 percent of the average school history, is seen as the best way to avoid sticky questions like women and sex mores, or the long and disgraceful history of organized religious opposition to women's rights and opportunities.

Yet nothing more clearly illustrates the paucity of research and information that typify these texts than discussions which take the upper-class Victorian matron (or the Gibson Girl or the Flapper) as *the* American woman of her time. While a minority may have sipped tea and embroidered flowers, the majority of American women toiled on the nation's farms or in the textile plants. Immigrant women wore out their lives in domestic service or in sweatshop tenements; slave women worked like cattle to bring in the cotton, rice, and indigo of the Old South. Chivalry, decorum, and all the trappings of the familiar "pedestal" of the nineteenth-century lady were no part of their lives. But their history, touching as it does on the heart of the country's economic, social, and cultural life, is omitted in favor of a few platitudes or silence.

The Housework Fallacy

Textbooks' treatment of women reflects cultural ideas of female inferiority as well as the notion that women's lives and interests are basically dependent upon those of some favored male. The implication is that women have never had any activities of interest or importance outside of traditional male preoccupations; within the male hierarchy, they have, of course, occupied mostly inferior positions.

There is a basic problem with this assumption; it is incorrect.

To illustrate this, let me select one area—some aspects of American economic history—and point out some of the facts, issues, and events ignored by the current population of textbook authors.

If you were to ask students what most American women have done during our history, I suspect that the answer would be "housework." That would be correct, yet what we today consider housework bears little resemblance in either extent or importance to the multitude of tasks performed by the colonial and frontier housewife, and indeed by the rural woman well into the twentieth century. In the colonies, on the frontier, and for the earlier part of the nineteenth century, most Americans lived on subsistence farms. Their families made almost everything they needed, and in the usual division of labor, the women of the family were responsible for the manifold manufac-turing processes needed to turn all raw materials of the farm into useable goods. This included everything from turning raw flax into clothes, processing all foods (includ-ing making butter, cheese, sausages, and preserving meats) to soap and candle making. The kitchen garden and livestock were also their responsibility. When this work was added to the laborious routine of cleaning, washing, and cooking, and to the burdens of maternity, nursing, and general child care, it is easy to see women's economic importance. It is also easy to see why numbers of women were prepared to farm and homestead independently. According to historian Robert Smutts, probably the largest group of nineteenth-century female proprietors were wo-men who claimed and worked their own land in the West.

The economic importance of the American woman was altered by the developments of the industrial revolution. The mechanization of home processes in the clothing industry, and later in baking, canning, and cooking, led to the devaluation of a woman's labor. Housework was suddenly worthless, and women and their children followed "women's work" out of the home and into the mills and factories.

Fragility and the 14-hour Day

There the "weak and fragile" creatures of Victorian sentiment were worked as long as 14 hours a day in cold, ill-ventilated, unhealthy barns, foul with dust, fibers, and chemicals. The old ideas of female inferiority now justified the lower wages of women operatives, with the result that they undercut men's wages, as their own were undermined by the pitiful salaries of the factory children. The availability of women and children for factory work was one of the important stimuli for industrialization in the East, and low wages and the long hours demanded of these operatives in effect subsidized the early industrial revolution in America.

The impact of the change in the locus of female labor, the conditions of early industrial revolution, the rationale for employing female and child labor, and the efforts of women as well as men to humanize the industrial system are all topics of real historical relevance. Yet if these changes receive as much as a paragraph, the author has been atypically generous.

Much of the widespread ignorance about the modern economic position of women may be traced to a similar disinterest in the later history of women in the labor force. Such changes as the rapid increase of women employed outside the home in the twentieth century, the mobilization of female labor during both world wars, and the beginnings of ideas about economic equality for women have had a vast impact on our economic structure. The history of women and work, including the trade union movement, and the social and cultural consequences of the American habit of using women as a pool of cheap expendable labor are certainly subjects properly in history texts and in materials prepared for social studies programs.

The economic aspect is not the only neglected facet of women's history. It is hard to get a complete picture of *any* topic in our history when half of the population is omitted from discussion. In addition to disregarding economic issues concerning women, the historical omissions and inaccuracies of the history textbooks usually encompass women's legal history; female contributions to art, science, and culture; ideas and theories about women; the women's movement; and birth control and changing sexual standards. While serious from a historical point of view, these distortions and omissions have another, perhaps even more important, impact upon students' views of women. It is a striking illustration of assumptions of female inferiority when publishers, writers, teachers, and parents accept materials that downgrade or ignore half or more of the consumers of text materials.

The treatment of American women in history texts is only one small facet in a pattern of sexism and racism. However, the history texts might make a real contribution to changing the image of American women and to improving the self-image of female students. It is hard to see how one can accept the idea that women are weak and frivolous after learning about the suffrage movement, the role of women in the industrial revolution, the tasks of frontier women, or the development of education for women of all races. It is very hard to see how women can be labeled "uncreative" and intellectually dependent after learning about the evolution of modern dance or of women's contributions to the performing and the visual arts. It is hard to imagine that students would uncritically accept the myths about women's intellectual capacities or personality after studying the pseudo-scientific theories marshalled to support them or the social, cultural, and religious prejudices which sustained the inferiority of women. If demanding that the nation's textbooks stop purveying myths and stereotypes in place of history cannot, by itself, alter ideas about women, at least textbook changes could prevent the transmission of blatant sexism and racism to another generation of American young people.

Starting Time		Finishing Time	
Reading Time		Reading Rate	
Comprehension		Vocabulary	

Comprehension— Read the following questions and statements. For each one, put an x in the box before the option that contains the most complete or accurate answer. Check your answers in the Answer Key on page 107.

1. Traditionally, American history textbooks have reflected
   ☐ a. a cultural historical view of women.
   ☐ b. an accurate view of women.
   ☐ c. a mythic historical view of women.
   ☐ d. a revolutionary view of women.

2. Those women who have earned a legitimate place in current history texts have had to
   ☐ a. lower their standards.
   ☐ b. meet masculine standards.
   ☐ c. champion controversial causes.
   ☐ d. provide comic relief.

3. The value of "housework" dropped
   ☐ a. as a result of a severe economic depression.
   ☐ b. during periods of war.
   ☐ c. as household chores became increasingly mechanized.
   ☐ d. as women sought fulfillment outside the home.

4. The position women occupy in society is clearly related to
   ☐ a. the level of education they achieve as a group.
   ☐ b. the decisions handed down by the Supreme Court.
   ☐ c. the role they played in history.
   ☐ d. the treatment given them in textbooks.

5. In their treatment of women, historians have preferred for the most part to
   ☐ a. ignore them completely.
   ☐ b. stress detail rather than substance.
   ☐ c. insist on their religious contributions.
   ☐ d. defend their right to be heard.

6. To the general public, the contributions of the women listed in this selection
   ☐ a. do not ring true.
   ☐ b. have always been known.
   ☐ c. confirm its suspicions.
   ☐ d. come as a surprise.

7. Which of the following would benefit the most from an improved image of women in history texts?
   ☐ a. politicians
   ☐ b. publishers
   ☐ c. writers
   ☐ d. the general public

8. The statement "Harriet Beecher Stowe, Harriet Tubman . . . are among the small and exclusive circle of women who are found deserving of a sentence or two," is
   ☐ a. sarcastic.
   ☐ b. humorous.
   ☐ c. inflammatory.
   ☐ d. pious.

9. The women most often portrayed in history textbooks are
   ☐ a. surly and defiant.
   ☐ b. silly and eccentric.
   ☐ c. strong and domineering.
   ☐ d. weak and confused.

10. The author uses the Gibson Girl as a symbol of
   ☐ a. the inner strength of all American women.
   ☐ b. underrated characters in American history.
   ☐ c. the frivolous nature of women.
   ☐ d. irrelevent characters in women's history.

Comprehension Skills

1. recalling specific facts	6. making a judgment
2. retaining concepts	7. making an inference
3. organizing facts	8. recognizing tone
4. understanding the main idea	9. understanding characters
5. drawing a conclusion	10. appreciation of literary forms

Study Skills, Part One—Following is a passage with blanks where words have been omitted. Next to the passage are groups of five words, one group for each blank. Complete the passage by selecting the correct word for each of the blanks.

Contextual Aids, III

6. Synonyms. Many times, unfamiliar words can be understood by noticing synonyms provided in the _____(1)_____. A synonym, as you recall, is a word with the same or nearly the same meaning as another word. The reader's task is to __(2)__ that a synonym is being given. With this knowledge, he can properly use the contextual aid. For example, a student reading the sentence *It was his custom never to be on time; he made a _ _ _ _ _ of tardiness* must recognize that the missing word is a synonym for *custom*. The word *habit* instantly comes to mind, __(3)__ the sentence perfectly. This contextual aid, too, is often found in textbook writing.

7. Setting the Mood. The setting or mood created by the context can __(4)__ to the reader the meaning of an unfamiliar word. In the sentence *It was a lovely _ _ _ _ _ scene, with snow blanketing the fields and trees* the setting is obviously *winter*. This would appear to be the word indicated by the context. Using setting and mood effectively requires imagery comprehension on the part of the reader; he must get the feeling or tone. Highly descriptive writing and poetry __(5)__ with this type of contextual aid.

8. Association. Certain words can arouse associations in the __(6)__ of the reader. These, in turn, serve as aids in order to recognize an unfamiliar word. The student reading the sentence *Turning their instruments, the _ _ _ _ _ awaited the appearance of the conductor* can see that the missing word is probably *musicians, band,* or *orchestra*. The words *tuning, instruments,* and *conductor* trigger the correct associations. The context of much of what we read provides __(7)__ for making associations like these.

(1)	dictionary		textbook
	context	index	mood

(2)	hope		disclose
	protest	report	discover

(3)	completing		commencing
	continuing	composing	containing

(4)	announce		suggest
	renounce	compare	confess

(5)	conflict		disagree
	identify	abound	dominate

(6)	mind		eye
	book	lesson	task

(7)	disappointments		surprises
	rewards	opportunities	struggles

Study Skills, Part Two—Read the study skills passage again, paying special attention to the lesson being taught. Then, without looking back at the passage, complete each sentence below by writing in the missing word or words. Check the Answer Key on page 107 for the answers to Study Skills, Part One, and Study Skills, Part Two.

1. A synonym is a word with the _____ meaning as another word.

2. Context sometimes creates a setting or _____ that can be used as a contextual aid.

3. Using this aid effectively requires the reader's understanding of _____ .

4. In descriptive writing and _____, tone is often used as a contextual aid.

5. Certain words trigger _____ in the mind of the reader that help him recognize unknown words.

12 Atlantis: Legend Lives On

by Arturo Gonzalez

Vocabulary—The five words below are from the story you are about to read. Study the words and their meanings. Then complete the ten sentences that follow, using one of the five words to fill in the blank in each sentence. Mark your answer by writing the letter of the word on the line before the sentence. Check your answers in the Answer Key on page 107.

A. impelled: driven; compelled

B. espouse: embrace; adopt a cause or belief

C. perpetrated: committed; carried out

D. intact: not damaged; whole

E. incongruities: inconsistencies; contradictions

_____ 1. There are only a few _____ between Plato's story of Atlantis and the theory of Galanopoulos and Bacon.

_____ 2. Several _____ frescoes have been discovered by researchers in Santorini.

_____ 3. Colonel Fawcett apparently felt _____ to go off in search of the legendary Atlantis.

_____ 4. One Nazi philosopher came to _____ the belief that Atlantans were the ancestors of the "superior Aryan race."

_____ 5. Researchers were delighted to find so many of Thera's physical structures _____ .

_____ 6. Through the years, unscrupulous characters have _____ hoaxes about Atlantis.

_____ 7. Zealots tend to overlook _____ in their theories.

_____ 8. Galanopoulos and Bacon _____ the belief that Santorini contained the lost city of Atlantis.

_____ 9. No one knows what heroic deeds might have been performed by Atlantans, or what crimes were _____ by them.

_____ 10. The mystery of Atlantis has _____ writers to devote huge amounts of time and energy to the subject.

Could it be that the lovely island of Santorini is the source of the mysterious legend of Atlantis?

"... There occurred violent earthquakes and floods, and in a single day and night of misfortune, all your war-like men in a body sank into the earth, and the island of Atlantis in like manner disappeared in the depths of the sea. For which reason the sea in those parts is impassable and impenetrable because there is a shoal of mud ..."

These words, written by Plato centuries ago, have sent expedition after expedition chasing down the world's most fascinating and intellectual archaeological detective story—what is the precise location of the lost land of Atlantis?

More than 5,000 books and tens of thousands of magazine and newspaper articles have been written on the subject. At least one scientific party, headed 30 years ago by a certain Colonel Fawcett from Britain, went deep into the Amazon jungle in search of Atlantis and has never been heard from again.

Atlantis is a legend which dies far more slowly than the mythical country itself expired. A convention of British journalists recently ranked a verifiable reemergence of Atlantis as one of the most important front-page stories newsmen could ever hope to write—far more compelling, in their professional opinion, than even the Second Coming of Christ. Such is the fascination of the unknown that in an era when hitting the moon with a manned expedition is a fait accompli, the thought of finding this lost land somewhere beneath the earth's endless ocean surface still captures our imagination with an intensity that few other concepts can match.

To study the alleged history of Atlantis is to journey back in time onto a magnificent continent of antiquity ... to hear the cry of vendors in the crowded markets of the capital city ... to listen to the clang of armor and weapons as imperial guards troop by ... to see the glitter of royal crowns amidst thousands of cheering subjects. This is the vision of bygone beauty which has impelled countless scholars and scientists to turn their backs on the magnificence of their labs in modern New York, their libraries in Paris, or colonnaded museums in Rome to devote a lifetime to the search for the dead, seaweed-encrusted remains of a lost, centuries-old continent—which indeed may never have existed.

These honest scientists are perhaps not the most fascinating Atlantis-seekers. Far more amusing are the theories of the charlatans, cosmologists, faith healers, and crackpots who over the years have seen Atlantis as a nondebatable historical proof for every variety of strange philosophy they may espouse. Atlantis attracts the kind of fanatics who spend their entire lives trying to prove that Bacon wrote Shakespeare's plays. The Atlantis theme has, over the years, been tied in a variety of ways to romanticism, racism, pacifism, theosophy, socialism, communism, and spiritualism. Crackpots have linked it with cannibalism, the Cyclops, and flying saucers as well.

A Russian cosmologist named Velikovsky insisted that Jupiter erupted millennia ago and spewed up a fiery comet which sped past the earth in 1600 or 1500 B.C., swamping Atlantis in the same roaring tide which parted the Red Sea and conveniently allowed the children of Israel to pass into the Promised Land. He explains that historians make no record of this event with the convenient rationale that the human race suffers from "collective amnesia."

The most monumental Atlantis hoax was perpetrated by Herman Schleimann who, in 1912, conned the *New York American* into running a lengthy feature story entitled "How I Discovered Atlantis, the Source of All Civilization." This not only sold newspapers to impressed New Yorkers by the thousands, but so befuddled the academic world that many texts and source books on the Atlantis legend still list facts and figures from Schleimann's daring piece of science fiction.

Atlantis has never yet been absolutely identified or pinpointed on the earth's surface. Numerous scientists have periodically amassed mounds of conflicting evidence to "definitely and indisputably" locate the mysterious continent variously in South, West, and North Africa, the Azores, the Canary Islands, the Caucasus, Ceylon, Spitsbergen, 13,000 feet up in the Andes, and in the Baltic Sea. Racial experts have credited Atlantis with fathering both the Spanish and the Italian races, and one of Hitler's hack philosophers in the Thirties actually tried to trace Aryan supremacy back to the glorious Atlantans, locating the island just a few miles off the Nazi coastline.

A few years ago no less than three costly expeditions were simultaneously exploring different world sites in a futile search for the remains of Atlantis. Depth charges and sonar were being bounced off the ocean bottom near the Azores; a descendant of Leon Trotsky was skin-diving off Bermuda in search of the lost country, while the *Discovery II,* a British research ship, charted the Galicia Bank, a steep-sided, 20-mile-long protuberance in the seabed 2,400 feet under the Atlantic's surface 30 miles off the coast of Spain, another alleged site of the lost continent.

Many experts insist on placing Atlantis midway in the Atlantic Ocean, claiming this location makes it a bridge between the Old World and the New and helps to explain some striking similarities between early Egyptian and American Indian cultures, as shown, for example, by the fondness each civilization had for pyramid-like structures.

But now, two scientists persuasively argue that Atlantis was not in the Atlantic at all, but was a Mediterranean island off the coast of Greece. In their book *Atlantis, the Truth Behind the Legend,* A. G. Galanopoulos and Edward Bacon present convincing evidence that the original Atlantis is really the Island of Santorini, 78 miles northeast of Crete. Atlantis, they insist, was really a Mediterranean/ Middle Eastern civilization—a culture mysteriously destroyed around 1500 B.C. They think they have even found a reason for its destruction: a massive volcanic eruption similar to the explosion which destroyed Krakatoa in Indonesia in 1883, which sent most of Santorini plunging under the sea and triggered huge tidal waves that swept up against Middle Eastern shorelines and through the Mediterranean, washing away life in the Minoan city of Knossos on Crete, just a little under 100 miles away.

There can be no doubt that Santorini was destroyed by a huge volcanic eruption in approximately 1450 B.C. Today, it remains as five islands, clearly composing the nearly perfectly circular walls and central cone of a volcano which has exploded and collapsed in on itself.

To understand how a single volcanic eruption could completely destroy a multi-island culture one has only to look at Krakatoa. When this volcano exploded in 1883, the explosion was heard 1,900 miles away and the sea was covered in pumice for more than 100 miles. So much ash went into the sky that sunsets around the world were extremely red for more than a year. It sent out tidal waves so large that ships at anchor in South America broke their mooring chains.

Using this as a yardstick, it's interesting to note that the Santorini explosion would have been three times as large. The Krakatoa blast destroyed only nine square miles of land; the Santorini explosion would have blown up more than 31 square miles.

The huge tidal waves it caused started floods as far away as Egypt, according to the legends of Manetho, and may have been the reason why Noah took to his ark. Its waves could have even been the reason the Red Sea opened up for Moses, and the iron oxide fallout from its smoke might have been the reason that the Bible says the Nile ran red. The tidal wave it caused definitely dropped pumice on the Jaffa shoreline 562 miles away, some 16½ feet above sea level.

One definite result of the eruption: it buried sections of Santorini beneath 100 feet of ash. And under this ash has recently been discovered a buried Minoan town, similar to the sophisticated civilization found on Crete, and quite probably the remains of the city of Atlantis which so fascinated the Greeks because it was so civilized and then disappeared so completely. The city—called Thera—was found by an American, James W. Mavor, Jr. of the Woods Hole Oceanographic Institute. He helped build the Alvin, the mini-sub that recovered the lost H-bomb off Spain, and several years ago cruised Santorini's central bay in the research ship *Chain,* using sonar to map the bottom and bringing up evidence that there was a major community destroyed by the volcanic explosion below. Actually, researchers have known that there was a community under both the bay and the shoreline for more than a century; during the construction of the Suez Canal, builders found that the ash from Thera made a high-quality, waterproof cement and in digging it up, first evidences of a city under it all came to light.

Now the village looks very much as if it is becoming an Eastern Mediterranean Pompeii, an intact city of two- and three-story houses apparently still standing under the ash. As one researcher summed it up, "We had expected to find the ruins of a prehistoric town. What surprised us was that it was three-dimensional. In most finds, the ruins don't come up to your knee. . . ." Even the frescoes, usually just piles of plaster on the floor by the time the archaeologists get to them, are beautifully preserved. The first nine trenches that were dug yielded enough artifacts to load down 35 donkeys. The absence of skeletons and gold suggests that the ancient inhabitants had some disaster warning, escaping in their boats and leaving houses and furniture sealed under the preserving ash for the scientists to find. A volcano which smoked for a few days before blowing up would have been enough to drive the frightened citizens away. Some refugees almost certainly went to Lebanon and Syria; some of today's Middle Easterners are thus Atlantans by heritage.

Where precise details on the Plato story of Atlantis and the current Cretan theory don't match exactly, there is also an explanation. Plato, after all, picked up the story, secondhand, from Solon who, in turn, got it from Egyptian priests, who had been handing it down verbally for a thousand years. Possible translations and misinterpretations of the legend help to explain away the few incongruities and even the incongruities are under investigation. A small team of researchers sponsored by the government of Greece and the Boston Museum of Fine Arts is working steadily away and recently a Professor Marinatos discovered some frescoes suggesting that the remains of a royal palace are not far off.

And so, the legend of Atlantis is moving from mystery to an Eastern Mediterranean fact. Now the big remaining, unsolved mystery is: whatever happened to Colonel Fawcett?

Starting Time		Finishing Time	
Reading Time		Reading Rate	
Comprehension		Vocabulary	

Comprehension— Read the following questions and statements. For each one, put an *x* in the box before the option that contains the most complete or accurate answer. Check your answers in the Answer Key on page 107.

1. Scholars and scientists who have searched for the lost city have been driven by
   □ a. the promise of wealth.
   □ b. creative genius.
   □ c. social pressures.
   □ d. a vision of beauty.

2. The author seems to support the theory that Atlantis is the sunken remains of
   □ a. Krakatoa.   □ c. the Azores.
   □ b. Pompeii.   □ d. Santorini.

3. The value of ash from Thera was discovered
   □ a. just before the establishment of the Woods Hole Oceanographic Institution.
   □ b. during the eruption of Krakatoa.
   □ c. during the building of the Suez Canal.
   □ d. soon after publication of *Atlantis, The Truth Behind the Legend.*

4. The dream of discovering the lost land of Atlantis
   □ a. remains as elusive as ever.
   □ b. may soon become a reality.
   □ c. has lost much of its glamour.
   □ d. attracts few legitimate scientists.

5. The reaction to Plato's account of the disappearance of Atlantis seems to justify the belief that it
   □ a. once existed.
   □ b. never existed.
   □ c. was destroyed by fire.
   □ d. was conquered by Greece.

6. Atlantis, the legend, has generated
   □ a. scientific conclusions.   □ c. weird theories.
   □ b. international unrest.   □ d. new religions.

7. The Russian cosmologist Velikovsky had
   □ a. access to many ancient documents.
   □ b. the respect of all his colleagues.
   □ c. severe doubts about the existence of Atlantis.
   □ d. no proof of his theory.

8. The tone of the opening paragraph is
   □ a. wistful.   □ c. dramatic.
   □ b. melancholy.   □ d. bland.

9. Galanopoulos and Bacon hope to
   □ a. convince the public that their theory is correct.
   □ b. live off the royalties made by their book.
   □ c. increase the tourist trade in and around Crete.
   □ d. earn the respect of Mediterranean specialists.

10. The selection is written in the form of
   □ a. an editorial.   □ c. an allegory.
   □ b. a report.   □ d. a document.

Comprehension Skills

1. recalling specific facts	6. making a judgment
2. retaining concepts	7. making an inference
3. organizing facts	8. recognizing tone
4. understanding the main idea	9. understanding characters
5. drawing a conclusion	10. appreciation of literary forms

Study Skills, Part One—Following is a passage with blanks where words have been omitted. Next to the passage are groups of five words, one group for each blank. Complete the passage by selecting the correct word for each of the blanks.

Contextual Aids, IV

9. Adjective Clauses. New words can be understood when ___(1)___ by adjective clauses. Frequently an unknown word modified by an adjective clause can be understood by the ___(2)___ contained in the clause. In the sentence *The _ _ _ _ _ which shine in the sky at night have always fascinated man,* the missing word is modified by an adjective clause. The same clause acts as a contextual aid, telling the reader that the missing word is *stars.*

10. Appositives. A word can be ___(3)___ and understood through another word used in apposition to it. A word in

(1)   expressed   explained
   interrupted   accompanied   contradicted

(2)   letters   associations
   comprehension   synonyms   information

(3)   found   enjoyed
   recognized   created   imagined

apposition is placed beside another word, further explaining it. Appositives give the reader a clue to the meaning of the unknown word. In the sentence _____, *policemen in plain clothes, joined the investigation,* the reader is informed by the appositive *policemen* that the missing word is probably *detectives.* Appositives are __(4)__ placed next to the word they explain. For this reason they are relatively easy to recognize and exploit as contextual aids.

11. Cause and Effect. Words can be understood through a cause-and-effect __(5)__ between the unknown word and other words in the sentence. The reader's understanding of the cause-effect pattern offers a clue to the meaning of the unknown words. In the sentence *Because they ate a hearty lunch just before swimming, many of the bathers suffered _____,* anyone who understands the __(6)__ of eating just before swimming knows that the missing word is *cramps.*

Discovering word meaning through context clues is not new to you; you have been using context intuitively all your life. However, as you __(7)__ more and more difficult words with subtler or complex meanings, you will come to realize that the use of context clues is one of your most powerful learning tools.

(4)   rarely   always
     sometimes   never   frequently

(5)   knowledge   pattern
  disagreement   relationship   understanding

(6)   distress   effects
      pain   causes   problem

(7)   discard   create
    encounter   use   overlook

Study Skills, Part Two—Read the study skills passage again, paying special attention to the lesson being taught. Then, without looking back at the passage, complete each sentence below by writing in the missing word or words. Check the Answer Key on page 107 for the answers to Study Skills, Part One, and Study Skills, Part Two.

1. New words can sometimes be understood from information contained in _____ clauses.

2. Another contextual aid is a word in _____ placed next to the unknown word.

3. Appositives _____ explain the words placed next to them.

4. Sometimes a reader's understanding of a cause- _____ pattern can help him to understand an unknown word.

5. Most of us have been using context clues _____ all of our lives.

13 | Police Brutality: Answers to Key Questions

by Albert J. Reiss, Jr.

Vocabulary—The five words below are from the story you are about to read. Study the words and their meanings. Then complete the ten sentences that follow, using one of the five words to fill in the blank in each sentence. Mark your answer by writing the letter of the word on the line before the sentence. Check your answers in the Answer Key on page 107.

A. precedent: previous example; custom

B. monitored: observed

C. insinuate: hint; imply

D. deprecate: belittle

E. predominated: showed greater power, importance, or quantity

_____ 1. Some critics _____ that police officers are simply thugs with badges.

_____ 2. Police say they have _____ the movement of idle black youths in order to curb crime.

_____ 3. On some police forces, there seems to be an established _____ for the use of brutality.

_____ 4. Outraged citizens feel the abusive language of police officers serves to _____ innocent minority citizens.

_____ 5. For the study, police activities were _____ for seven weeks.

_____ 6. High crime rates have traditionally _____ in areas of low socio-economic status.

_____ 7. The records show that police brutality _____ in certain areas as far back as 1903.

_____ 8. In engaging in excessive violence, police are adhering to a long-standing _____ .

_____ 9. Some police tactics seem designed to _____ suspects in the eyes of the community.

_____ 10. Police _____ that loitering leads to crime.

Can we agree on a definition of brutality?

For three years, there has been through the courts and the streets a dreary procession of citizens with broken heads and bruised bodies against few of whom was violence needed to effect an arrest. Many of them had done nothing to deserve an arrest. In a majority of such cases, no complaint was made. If the victim complains, his charge is generally dismissed. The police are practically above the law."

The statement was published in 1903, and its author was the Hon. Frank Moss, a former police commissioner of New York City. Clearly, today's charges of police brutality and mistreatment of citizens have a precedent in American history—but never before has the issue of police brutality assumed the public urgency it has today. In Newark, in Detroit, in Watts, in Harlem, and, in fact, in practically every city that has had a civil disturbance, "deep hostility between police and ghetto" was, reports the Kerner Commission, "a primary cause of the riots."

Whether or not the police accept the words "police brutality," the public now wants some plain answers to some plain questions. How widespread is police mistreatment of citizens? Is it on the increase? Why do policemen mistreat citizens? Do the police mistreat blacks more than whites?

To find some answers, 36 people working for the Center for Research on Social Organization observed police-citizen encounters in the cities of Boston, Chicago, and Washington, D.C. For seven days a week, for seven weeks, these observers, with police permission, sat in patrol cars and monitored booking and lockup procedures in high-crime precincts.

Obtaining information about police mistreatment of citizens is no simple matter. National and state civil-rights commissions receive hundreds of complaints charging mistreatment—but proving these allegations is difficult. The few local civilian-review boards, such as the one in Philadelphia, have not produced any significant volume of complaints leading to the dismissal or disciplining of policemen for alleged brutality. Generally, police chiefs are silent on the matter, or answer charges of brutality with vague statements that they will investigate any complaints brought to their attention. Rank-and-file policemen are usually more outspoken: They often insinuate that charges of brutality are part of a conspiracy against them, and against law and order.

The Meaning of Brutality

What citizens mean by police brutality covers the full range of police practices. These practices, contrary to the impression of many civil-rights activists, are not newly devised to deal with blacks in our urban ghettos. They are ways in which the police have traditionally behaved in dealing with certain citizens, particularly those in the lower classes. The most common of these practices are:
- the use of profane and abusive language,
- commands to move on or get home,
- stopping and questioning people on the street or searching them and their cars,
- threats to use force if not obeyed,
- prodding with a nightstick or approaching with a pistol, and
- the actual use of physical force or violence itself.

Citizens and the police do not always agree on what constitutes proper police practice. What is "proper," or what is "brutal," it need hardly be pointed out, is more a matter of judgment about what someone did than a description of what police do. What is important is not the practice itself but what it means to the citizen. What citizens object to and call "police brutality" is really the judgment that they have not been treated with the full rights and dignity owing citizens in a democratic society. Any practice that degrades their status, that restricts their freedom, that annoys or harasses them, or that uses physical force is frequently seen as unnecessary and unwarranted. More often than not, they are probably right.

Many police practices serve only to degrade the citizen's sense of himself and his status. This is particularly true with regard to the way the police use language. Most citizens who have contact with the police object less to their use of four-letter words than to *how* the policeman talks to them. Particularly objectionable is the habit policemen have of "talking down" to citizens, of calling them names that deprecate them in their own eyes and those of others. More than one black citizen has complained: "They talk down to me as if I had no name— like 'boy' or 'Man' or whatever, or they call me 'Jack' or by my first name. They don't show me no respect."

To be treated as "suspicious" is not only degrading, but is also a form of harassment and a restriction on the right to move freely. The harassing tactics of many policemen—dispersing social street-gatherings, the indiscriminate stopping of blacks on foot or in cars, and commands to move on or go home—are particularly common in ghetto areas.

Young people are the most likely targets of harassing orders to disperse or move on. Particularly in summer, ghetto youths are likely to spend lots of time in public places. Given the inadequacy of their housing and the absence of community facilities, the street corner is often their social center. As the police cruise the busy streets of the ghetto, they frequently shout at groups of teenagers to "get going" or "get home." Our observations of police practices show that *white as well as black youths* are often harassed in this way.

Frequently the policeman may leave the car and threaten or force youths to move on. For example, one summer evening as the scout car cruised a busy street of a white slum, the patrolman observed three white boys and a girl on a corner. When told to move on, they mumbled and grumbled in undertones, angering the police by their failure to comply. As they slowly moved off, the officers pushed them along the street. Suddenly one of the white patrolmen took a lighted cigarette from a 15-year-old boy and stuck it in his face, pushing him forward as he did so. When the youngsters did move on, one policeman remarked to the observer that the girl was "nothing but a whore." Such tactics can only intensify resentment toward the police.

Police harassment is not confined to youth. One in every four adult blacks in Detroit claims he has been stopped and questioned by the police without good reason. The same proportion claim they have been stopped in their cars. One in five says he has been searched unnecessarily; and one in six says that his car was searched for no good reason. The members of an interracial couple, particularly a black man accompanying a white woman, are perhaps the most vulnerable to harassment.

What citizens regard as police brutality many policemen consider necessary for law enforcement. While degrading epithets and abusive language may no longer be considered proper by either police commanders or citizens, they often disagree about other practices related to law enforcement. For example, although many citizens see "stop and question" or "stop and frisk" procedures as harassment, police commanders usually regard them merely as "aggressive prevention" to curb crime.

Physical Force—or Self-Defense?

The nub of the police-brutality issue seems to lie in police use of physical force. By law, the police have the right to use such force if necessary to make an arrest, to keep the peace, or to maintain public order. But just how much force is necessary or proper?

This was the crucial problem we attempted to answer by placing observers in the patrol cars and in the precincts. Our 36 observers, divided equally between Chicago, Boston, and Washington, were responsible for reporting the details of all situations where police used physical force against a citizen. To ensure the observation of a large number of encounters, two high-crime police precincts were monitored in Boston and in Chicago; four in Washington. At least one precinct was composed of primarily black residents, another primarily whites. Where possible, we also tried to select precincts with considerable variation in social-class composition. Given the criterion of a high-crime rate, however, people of low socioeconomic status predominated in most of the areas surveyed.

The law fails to provide simple rules about what—and how much—force that policemen can properly use. The

American Bar Foundation's study *Arrest,* by Wayne La Fave, puts the matter rather well, stating that the courts of all states would undoubtedly agree that in making an arrest a policeman should use only that amount of force he reasonably believes necessary. But La Fave also pointed out that there is no agreement on the question of when it is better to let the suspect escape than to employ "deadly" force.

Even in those states where the use of deadly force is limited by law, the kinds of physical force a policeman may use are not clearly defined. No kind of force is categorically denied a policeman, since he is always permitted to use deadly force in self-defense.

This right to protect himself often leads the policeman to argue self-defense whenever he uses force. We found that many policemen, whether or not the facts justify it, regularly follow their use of force with the charge that the citizen was assaulting a policeman or resisting arrest. Our observers also found that some policemen even carry pistols and knives that they have confiscated while searching citizens; they carry them so they may be placed at a scene should it be necessary to establish a case of self-defense.

Of course, not all cases of force involve the use of *unnecessary* force. Each instance of force reported by our observers was examined and judged to be either necessary or unnecessary. Cases involving simple restraint—holding a man by the arm—were deliberately excluded from consideration, even though a policeman's right to do so can, in many instances, be challenged. In judging when police force is "unwarranted," "unreasonable," or "undue," we rather deliberately selected only those cases in which a policeman struck the citizen with his hands, fist, feet, or body, or where he used a weapon of some kind—such as a nightstick or a pistol. In these cases, had the policeman been found to have used physical force improperly, he could have been arrested on complaint and, like any other citizen, charged with a simple or aggravated assault. A physical assault on a citizen was judged to be "improper" or "unecessary" only if force was used in one or more of the following ways:

- If a policeman physically assaulted a citizen and then failed to make an arrest; proper use involves an arrest.
- If the citizen being arrested did not, by word or deed, resist the policeman; force should be used only if it is necessary to make the arrest.
- If the policeman, even though there was resistance to the arrest, could easily have restrained the citizen in other ways.
- If a large number of policemen were present and could have assisted in subduing the citizen in the station, in lockup, and in the interrogation rooms.
- If an offender was handcuffed and made no attempt to flee or offer violent resistance.
- If the citizen resisted arrest, but the use of force continued even after the citizen was subdued.

In the seven-week period, we found 37 cases in which

force was used improperly. In all, 44 citizens had been assaulted. In 15 of these cases, no one was arrested. Of these, 8 had offered no verbal or physical resistance whatsoever, while 7 had.

An arrest was made in 22 of the cases. In 13, force was exercised in the station house when at least four other policemen were present. In two cases, there was no verbal or physical resistance to the arrest but force was still applied. In two other cases, the police applied force to a handcuffed offender in a field setting. And in five

situations, the offender did resist arrest, but the policemen continued to use force even after he had been subdued.

Starting Time		Finishing Time	
Reading Time		Reading Rate	
Comprehension		Vocabulary	

Comprehension— Read the following questions and statements. For each one, put an *x* in the box before the option that contains the most complete or accurate answer. Check your answers in the Answer Key on page 107.

1. The relationship between crime and poor living conditions is
   - ☐ a. not convincing.
   - ☐ b. totally absent.
   - ☐ c. low.
   - ☐ d. high.

2. Police feel that aggressive tactics are
   - ☐ a. outdated and unnecessary.
   - ☐ b. the quickest path to promotion.
   - ☐ c. legal but unethical.
   - ☐ d. justified in the name of crime prevention.

3. Police officers should use force
   - ☐ a. whenever a suspect looks dangerous.
   - ☐ b. when a suspect resists arrest.
   - ☐ c. only in interrogation rooms.
   - ☐ d. only after reading a suspect his rights.

4. All police enforcement agencies would do well to
   - ☐ a. treat suspects politely and patiently.
   - ☐ b. hesitate before making an arrest.
   - ☐ c. respect a suspect's self-image.
   - ☐ d. avoid the use of undercover procedures.

5. The relationship between police brutality and civil disobedience is
   - ☐ a. uncertain.
   - ☐ b. unknown.
   - ☐ c. absent.
   - ☐ d. direct.

6. The answer to the question, "How much physical force should be used by the police?" is often
   - ☐ a. a matter of careful thought.
   - ☐ b. a question of conscience.
   - ☐ c. a decision reached by all policemen.
   - ☐ d. an interpretation of a legal definition.

7. The definition of what constitutes police brutality often depends on
   - ☐ a. police reports.
   - ☐ b. subjective interpretation.
   - ☐ c. eyewitnesses.
   - ☐ d. medical testimony.

8. The first paragraph
   - ☐ a. is an irresponsible statement.
   - ☐ b. defends the actions of the police.
   - ☐ c. accuses the public of indifference.
   - ☐ d. sets the tone of the selection.

9. Many black citizens feel
   - ☐ a. unfairly singled out as targets of police brutality.
   - ☐ b. ashamed by the behavior of black police officers.
   - ☐ c. unnerved by the increase in violent crimes.
   - ☐ d. police harassment is the price they must pay if they wish to live in the city.

10. The sentence "When told to move on, they mumbled and grumbled in undertones, angering the police by their failure to comply" is an example of
    - ☐ a. figurative language.
    - ☐ b. literal language.
    - ☐ c. symbolic language.
    - ☐ d. imaginative language.

Comprehension Skills

1. recalling specific facts	6. making a judgment
2. retaining concepts	7. making an inference
3. organizing facts	8. recognizing tone
4. understanding the main idea	9. understanding characters
5. drawing a conclusion	10. appreciation of literary forms

Study Skills, Part One—Following is a passage with blanks where words have been omitted. Next to the passage are groups of five words, one group for each blank. Complete the passage by selecting the correct word for each of the blanks.

Reviewing for Examinations, I

For many students, the expression "Into every life a little rain must fall" pertains to the inevitability of final examinations. Although many schools are adopting pass-fail ___(1)___ for courses, and others are revising the portion of final grade based on examinations, most students will be taking exams for most courses. Face it—exams are a fact of academic life.

Unfortunately (and unnecessarily), many students ___(2)___ at examination time. They worry so much that they cannot study and review effectively. This results in ___(3)___ performance on the test and causes even more apprehension on future tests. You must break the cycle. Success on your next set of finals can ___(4)___ the process.

The main reason students panic is lack of adequate preparation. To most students, final review means cramming—a do-or-die, headlong plunge into the unfamiliar waters of the subject matter. Cramming can be beneficial; any brief, intensive review is sure to do more good than harm. As your only method of exam ___(5)___ however, cramming lets you down. There's just too much to be covered.

Successful preparation has two prerequisites: suitable notes and continuous review. You cannot begin to study well with unsatisfactory notes. In addition to knowing what is in the text, you must be able to recall and review what was ___(6)___ in class. You need a good set of notes to do this.

You must review ___(7)___ and faithfully all through the term, not just before exams. This approach will not only ease the load at exam time, but will also lead to a better understanding of the subject matter with each review.

(1)	answers	grades
	outlines standards	guidelines
(2)	panic	rest
	study review	relax
(3)	improved	fair
	excellent poor	definite
(4)	improve	reinforce
	advance reverse	deny
(5)	organization	repetition
	instruction administration	preparation
(6)	rejected	introduced
	emphasized omitted	approached
(7)	finally	initially
	happily rarely	regularly

Study Skills, Part Two—Read the study skills passage again, paying special attention to the lesson being taught. Then, without looking back at the passage, complete each sentence below by writing in the missing word or words. Check the Answer Key on page 107 for the answers to Study Skills, Part One, and Study Skills, Part Two.

1. Successful examination preparation includes good _____ and continuous review.

2. Too much worry can result in poor _____ results.

3. Cramming should not be your only _____ of test preparation.

4. In addition to material from the text, you must review important notes from _____ .

5. Better understanding of the subject matter is accomplished with each _____ .

14 | **The Interlopers**

by Saki

Vocabulary—The five words below are from the story you are about to read. Study the words and their meanings. Then complete the ten sentences that follow, using one of the five words to fill in the blank in each sentence. Mark your answer by writing the letter of the word on the line before the sentence. Check your answers in the Answer Key on page 108.

A. afforded: provided

B. acquiesced: complied or accepted without protest

C. wont: accustomed

D. languor: lack of physical or mental energy

E. succor: relief; assistance

_____ 1. The predicament in which the two men found themselves _____ them time to rethink their attitudes.

_____ 2. Ulrich decided to have his men offer _____ to Georg.

_____ 3. Both the von Gradwitz family and the Znaeym family were _____ to hold a grudge.

_____ 4. The wine flask _____ Ulrich some measure of comfort.

_____ 5. Because Ulrich was trapped under the tree, he could not provide _____ to Georg.

_____ 6. Ulrich felt confident that his men would have _____ in his plan to end the feud.

_____ 7. The Znaeym family had never _____ in the legal ruling pertaining to the forest.

_____ 8. As they lay under the tree, both Ulrich and Georg felt pain and _____ setting in.

_____ 9. As _____ crept over him, Ulrich lost his hatred for Georg.

_____ 10. Roebuck are _____ to hide in hollows during wind storms.

In a forest of mixed growth somewhere on the eastern spurs of the Carpathians a man stood one winter night watching and listening, as though he waited for some beast of the woods to come within the range of his vision and, later, of his rifle. But the game for whose presence he kept so keen an outlook was none that figured in the sportsman's calendar

The two enemies glared at one another. Each had a rifle in his hand; each had murder in his mind.

as lawful and proper for the chase; Ulrich von Gradwitz patrolled the dark forest in quest of a human enemy.

The forest lands of Gradwitz were of wide extent and well-stocked with game; the narrow strip of precipitous woodland that lay on its outskirt was not remarkable for the game it harbored or the shooting it afforded, but it was the most jealously guarded of all its owner's territorial possessions. A famous lawsuit in the days of his grandfather had wrested it from the illegal possession of a neighboring family of petty landowners; the dispossessed party had never acquiesced in the judgment of the courts, and a long series of poaching affrays and similar scandals had embittered the relationships between the families for three generations. The neighbor feud had grown into a personal one since Ulrich had come to be head of his family; if there was a man in the world whom he detested and wished ill to, it was Georg Znaeym, the inheritor of the quarrel and the tireless game-snatcher and raider of the disputed border-forest.

The feud might, perhaps, have died down or been compromised if the personal ill will of the two men had not stood in the way: as boys they had thirsted for one another's blood, as men each prayed that misfortune might fall on the other; and this wind-scourged winter night Ulrich had banded together his foresters to watch the dark forest, not in quest of four-footed quarry, but to keep a lookout for the prowling thieves whom he suspected of being afoot from across the land boundary. The roebuck, which usually kept in the sheltered hollows during a storm wind, were running like driven things tonight, and there was movement and unrest among the creatures that were wont to sleep through the dark hours. Assuredly there was a disturbing element in the forest, and Ulrich could guess the quarter from whence it came.

He strayed away by himself from the watchers whom he had placed in ambush on the crest of the hill, and wandered far down the steep slopes amid the wild tangle of undergrowth, peering through the tree trunks and listening through the whistling and skirling of the wind and the restless beating of the branches for sight or sound of the marauders. If only on this wild night, in this dark, lone spot, he might come across Georg Znaeym man to man, with none to witness—that was the wish that was uppermost in his thoughts.

And as he stepped round the trunk of a huge beech, he came face to face with the man he sought.

The two enemies stood glaring at one another for a long, silent moment. Each had a rifle in his hand; each had hate in his heart and murder uppermost in his mind. The chance had come to give full play to the passions of a lifetime. But a man who had been brought up under the code of a restraining civilization cannot easily nerve himself to shoot down his neighbor in cold blood and without word spoken, except for an offense against his hearth and honor. And before the moment of hesitation had given way to action, a deed of Nature's own violence overwhelmed them both.

A fierce shriek of the storm had been answered by a splitting crash over their heads, and ere they could leap aside, a mass of falling beech tree had thundered down on them. Ulrich von Gradwitz found himself stretched on the ground, one arm numb beneath him and the other held almost as helplessly in a tight tangle of forked branches, while both legs were pinned beneath the fallen mass. His heavy shooting boots had saved his feet from being crushed to pieces, but if his fractures were not as serious as they might have been, at least it was evident that he could not move from his present position till someone came to release him. The descending twigs had slashed the skin of his face, and he had to wink away some drops of blood from his eyelashes before he could take in a general view of the disaster. At his side, so near that under ordinary circumstances he could almost have touched him, lay Georg Znaeym, alive and struggling but obviously as helplessly pinioned down as himself. All round them lay a thick-strewn wreckage of splintered branches and broken twigs.

Relief at being alive and exasperation at his captive plight brought a strange medley of pious thank-offerings and sharp curses to Ulrich's lips.

Georg, who was nearly blinded with the blood which trickled across his eyes, stopped his struggling for a moment to listen, and then gave a short, snarling laugh. "So you're not killed, as you ought to be, but you're caught anyway," he cried, "caught fast! Ho, what a jest— Ulrich von Gradwitz snarled in his stolen forest. There's real justice for you!" And he laughed again, mockingly and savagely.

"I'm caught in my own forest land," retorted Ulrich. "When my men come to release us, you will wish, perhaps, that you were in a better plight than caught poaching on a neighbor's land—shame on you!"

Georg was silent for a moment; then he answered quietly: "Are you sure that your men will find much to release? I have men, too, in the forest tonight, close behind me, and *they* will be here first and do the releasing. When they drag me out from under these branches, it won't need much clumsiness on their part to roll this mass of trunk right over on the top of you. Your men will find you dead under a fallen beech tree. For form's sake I shall send my condolences to your family."

"It is a useful hint," said Ulrich fiercely. "My men had orders to follow in ten minutes' time—seven of which must have gone by already—and when they get me out, I will remember the hint. Only, as you will have met your death poaching on my lands, I don't think I can decently send any message of condolence to your family."

"Good," snarled Georg, "good. We fight this quarrel out to the death, you and I and our foresters, with no cursed interlopers to come between us. Death and damnation to you, Ulrich von Gradwitz."

"The same to you, Georg Znaeym, forest-thief, game-snatcher."

Both men spoke with the bitterness of possible defeat before them, for each knew that it might be long before his men would seek him out or find him; it was a bare matter of chance which party would arrive first on the scene.

Both had now given up the useless struggle to free themselves from the mass of wood that held them down; Ulrich limited his endeavors to an effort to bring his one partially free arm near enough to his outer coat pocket to draw out his wine flask. Even when he had accomplished that operation, it was long before he could manage the unscrewing of the stopper or get any of the liquid down his throat. But what a heaven-sent draft it seemed! It was an open winter, and little snow had fallen as yet; hence the captives suffered less from the cold than might have been the case at that season of the year; nevertheless, the wine was warming and reviving to the wounded man, and he looked across with something like a throb of pity to where his enemy lay, just keeping the groans of pain and weariness from crossing his lips.

"Could you reach this flask if I threw it over to you?" asked Ulrich suddenly. "There is good wine in it, and one may as well be as comfortable as one can. Let us drink, even if tonight one of us dies."

"No, I can scarcely see anything, there is so much blood caked round my eyes," said Georg, "and in any case I don't drink wine with an enemy."

Ulrich was silent for a few minutes, and lay listening to the weary screeching of the wind. An idea was slowly forming and growing in his brain, an idea that gained strength every time that he looked across at the man who was fighting so grimly against pain and exhaustion. In the pain and languor that Ulrich himself was feeling, the old fierce hatred seemed to be dying down.

"Neighbor," he said presently, "do as you please if your men come first. It was a fair compact. But as for me, I've changed my mind. If my men are the first to come, you shall be the first to be helped, as though you were my guest. We have quarreled like devils all our lives over this stupid strip of forest, where the trees can't even stand upright in a breath of wind. Lying here tonight, thinking, I've come to think we've been rather fools; there are better things in life than getting the better of a boundary dispute. Neighbor, if you will help me to bury the old quarrel, I—I will ask you to be my friend."

Georg Znaeym was silent for so long that Ulrich thought perhaps he had fainted with the pain of his injuries. Then he spoke slowly and in jerks. "How the whole region would stare and gabble if we rode into the market square together. No one living can remember seeing a Znaeym and a von Gradwitz talking to one another in friendship. And what peace there would be among the forester folk if we ended our feud tonight. And if we chose to make peace among our people, there is none other to interfere, no interlopers from outside. You would come and keep the Sylvester night beneath my roof, and I would come and feast on some high day at your castle. I would never fire a shot on your land save when you invited me as a guest, and you should come and shoot with me down in the marshes where the wild-fowl are. In all the countryside there are none that could hinder if we willed to make peace. I never thought to have wanted to do other than hate you all my life, but I think I have changed my mind about things too this last half hour. And you offered me your wine flask. Ulrich von Gradwitz, I will be your friend."

For a space both men were silent, turning over in their minds the wonderful changes that this dramatic reconciliation would bring about. In the cold, gloomy forest, with the wind tearing in fitful gusts through the naked branches and whistling round the tree trunks, they lay and waited for the help that would now bring release and succor to both parties. And each prayed a private prayer that his men might be the first to arrive, so that he might be the first to show honorable attention to the enemy that had become a friend.

Presently, as the wind dropped for a moment, Ulrich broke silence. "Let's shout for help," he said. "In this lull our voices may carry a little way."

"They won't carry far through the trees and undergrowth," said Georg, "but we can try. Together, then."

The two raised their voices in a prolonged hunting call.

"Together again," said Ulrich a few minutes later, after listening in vain for an answering hallo. "I heard something that time, I think," said Ulrich.

"I heard nothing but the pestilential wind," said Georg hoarsely.

There was silence again for some minutes, and then Ulrich gave a joyful cry. "I can see figures coming through the wood. They are following in the way I came down the hillside."

Both men raised their voices in as loud a shout as they could muster.

"They hear us! They've stopped. Now they see us. They're running down the hill towards us," cried Ulrich.

"How many of them are there?" asked Georg.

"I can't see distinctly," said Ulrich. "Nine or ten."

"Then they are yours," said Georg. "I had only seven out with me.

"They are making all the speed they can, brave lads," said Ulrich gladly.

"Are they your men?" asked Georg. "Are they your men?" he repeated impatiently, as Ulrich did not answer.

"No," said Ulrich with a laugh, the idiotic chattering laugh of a man unstrung with hideous fear.

"Who are they?" asked Georg quickly, straining his eyes to see what the other would gladly not have seen.

"Wolves."

H. H. Munro is a British writer who wrote under the pen name Saki. He is best known for his many witty short stories and his satirical writings about British society of the early 1900s. Born in Akyab, Burma, in 1870, Munro came to England when he was two years old and later became a well-known London journalist. In 1916 he was killed in a battle in France during World War I.

Starting Time		Finishing Time	
Reading Time		Reading Rate	
Comprehension		Vocabulary	

Comprehension

Comprehension— Read the following questions and statements. For each one, put an *x* in the box before the option that contains the most complete or accurate answer. Check your answers in the Answer Key on page 108.

1. Ulrich had instructed his men to
   - ☐ a. wait ten minutes, then come looking for him.
   - ☐ b. stand guard on the crest of the hill.
   - ☐ c. shoot prowling wolves on sight.
   - ☐ d. send condolences to the Znaeym family.

2. The narrow strip of woodland on the outskirts of von Gradwitz's property was
   - ☐ a. a popular hunting area.
   - ☐ b. an old bone of contention.
   - ☐ c. off-limits to von Gradwitz.
   - ☐ d. well-stocked with game.

3. The first indication of a change in von Gradwitz's attitude toward Znaeym occurred
   - ☐ a. when the tree fell.
   - ☐ b. after he drank from his flask.
   - ☐ c. when he offered his flask.
   - ☐ d. after Znaeym fainted.

4. Another title for this selection could be
   - ☐ a. The Revenge.
   - ☐ b. The Storm.
   - ☐ c. The Hunt.
   - ☐ d. The Encounter.

5. The hatred these two men have for each other
   - ☐ a. causes others to respect them.
   - ☐ b. sours their lives and affects others.
   - ☐ c. encourages others to cheat and steal.
   - ☐ d. began long ago as friendship.

6. The dramatic reconciliation was prompted by
   - ☐ a. financial reasons.
   - ☐ b. the fear of death.
   - ☐ c. a shared disaster.
   - ☐ d. religious considerations.

7. The activity of the roebuck on this windy winter night suggested the
   - ☐ a. start of the mating season.
   - ☐ b. abundance of small game.
   - ☐ c. threat of a fire.
   - ☐ d. presence of intruders.

8. Helpless and seriously hurt himself, Georg Znaeym's first reaction to von Gradwitz's plight was
   - ☐ a. bitter and sarcastic.
   - ☐ b. conciliatory.
   - ☐ c. quick and unexpected.
   - ☐ d. terrified.

9. Nature is portrayed as
   - ☐ a. capricious.
   - ☐ b. kind.
   - ☐ c. inconsistent.
   - ☐ d. ineffectual.

10. The sentence "The two enemies stood glaring at one another for a long, silent moment" is an example of
    - ☐ a. figurative language.
    - ☐ b. literal language.
    - ☐ c. imaginative description.
    - ☐ d. personification.

Comprehension Skills

1. recalling specific facts	6. making a judgment
2. retaining concepts	7. making an inference
3. organizing facts	8. recognizing tone
4. understanding the main idea	9. understanding characters
5. drawing a conclusion	10. appreciation of literary forms

Study Skills, Part One—Following is a passage with blanks where words have been omitted. Next to the passage are groups of five words, one group for each blank. Complete the passage by selecting the correct word for each of the blanks.

Reviewing for Examinations, II

Reviewing sounds like a lot of extra work, but it actually makes your life much easier. By keeping up with your work, you are more relaxed and more ___(1)___ . You will actually save time in the long run.

If you have not been reviewing during the term, start now. It will probably be necessary for you to outline the course to date; this is the best way to be sure you have covered everything. Schedule a week for the ___(2)___ and review and outline a segment each night. Anticipate as much reviewing as possible now.

With these two conditions in order, you are ready to get down to the business of studying for final exams.

STUDYING FOR FINALS

1. Establish a Review Schedule. As you have learned from working with your regular study schedule, you must be ___(3)___ to study successfully. Set up a new schedule a week or two before final exams, spreading the material to be reviewed and studied over the allotted time. Save the ___(4)___ day (the night before the actual test) for cramming; we'll see later how to cram intelligently. Divide the course work among the other days so that every aspect of the subject can be ___(5)___ .

Assign a reasonable length of time to your daily study period. If a subject is one of your "good" ones, an hour a day of concentrated study might be ___(6)___ . If, on the other hand, this subject has been giving you trouble, you will need to devote more time to it. Schedule accordingly.

Draw up your review schedule on paper, showing the ___(7)___ allotment each day for the subject. Obviously, for the system to work, you must spend the full time in actual study.

(1)	confident		expressive
	attractive	intelligent	friendly
(2)	vacation		task
	entertainment	family	introduction
(3)	clever		advanced
	cheerful	organized	original
(4)	initial		easiest
	first	final	best
(5)	covered		omitted
	approached	inspected	rejected
(6)	enjoyed		extravagant
	unwanted	unwise	sufficient
(7)	time		money
	food	space	clothes

Study Skills, Part Two—Read the study skills passage again, paying special attention to the lesson being taught. Then, without looking back at the passage, complete each sentence below by writing in the missing word or words. Check the Answer Key on page 108 for the answers to Study Skills, Part One, and Study Skills, Part Two.

1. Keeping up with your work can actually _____ you time.

2. The best way to be sure that you cover everything in a review is to

   _____ the course to date.

3. When you set up your study schedule, _____ the material to be

   reviewed over the alloted time.

4. The night before the test should be devoted to intelligent _____ .

5. The full time planned for review each night must be spent in actual _____ .

15 | The Plight of the Porpoise

by Robert Benkovitch

Vocabulary—The five words below are from the story you are about to read. Study the words and their meanings. Then complete the ten sentences that follow, using one of the five words to fill in the blank in each sentence. Mark your answer by writing the letter of the word on the line before the sentence. Check your answers in the Answer Key on page 108.

A. marauding: raiding

B. agility: quickness; nimbleness

C. aquatic: of or in water

D. depicted: pictured; portrayed

E. desultory: disconnected; haphazard

_____ 1. Each year thousands of tourists pay to see _____ mammals perform tricks in marinelands and oceanariums.

_____ 2. The Japanese have often been _____ as the leading killers of porpoises.

_____ 3. The _____ of porpoises is well established.

_____ 4. Porpoises use their _____ to protect themselves against sharks.

_____ 5. Unlike sharks, porpoises are not _____ creatures.

_____ 6. Yvonne Vladislavich believes she was saved from death by two _____ friends.

_____ 7. Federal and state regulations concerning killing porpoises are enforced in a _____ manner.

_____ 8. The 1972 Federal Marine Mammal Protection Act prevented _____ fishermen from intentionally killing porpoises.

_____ 9. Old sea tales often _____ porpoises as heroes and rescuers.

_____ 10. Porpoises seem to have the mental capacity to do more than simply execute _____ tricks.

If porpoises are intelligent, they will soon discover who their real enemies are.

Drifting in the warm shark-infested waters of the Indian Ocean on a Sunday in 1971, a cabin cruiser with a stalled engine was suddenly struck by a huge wave, overturned, and immediately sank. Three persons drowned as a result, but a determined 23-year-old Yvonne Vladislavich, with an open cut on her foot, began to swim toward the coast. A half dozen marauding sharks picked up the scent of blood and were soon trailing her. As the sharks began circling toward their prey, two porpoises suddenly appeared at her side. The sharks, knowing the speed and agility of their natural enemy, withdrew.

Miss Vladislavich, a strong swimmer, had a 25-mile distance ahead of her before reaching safety. Her strength began failing, but the porpoises helped her stay afloat. Eventually she reached a buoy, climbed on, and waited to be rescued.

Miss Vladislavich insists that she owes her life to the two porpoises—but their lives, unfortunately, may now be in the hands of man and his modern technology.

For centuries, porpoises have been recognized as man's closest aquatic friend. Briny tales have passed from sailor to sailor, telling how they guided lost boats through dense fog, or of rescuing drowning swimmers from dangerous waters. Even early Greek pottery often depicted a human riding on the back of a smiling porpoise.

One Greek myth suggests that some porpoises were once men. The story claims that Dionysus, the god of wine, was kidnapped and taken out to sea. When he realized his fate, the god made the boat's mast sprout grapevines. As the fearful and panic-stricken crew jumped overboard, Dionysus changed them into porpoises and forced the evil sailors to remain in the sea forever.

Evolutionary theory, based on studies done with fossil skeletons, slightly supports the ancient Greek tale—but only to the point that porpoises were once land-dwelling animals. Fifty million years ago, after adapting to life on land, the early ancestors of porpoises gave today's scientists a genuine mystery by returning to the sea. Although the real reason remains unknown, practicality appears to be the only explanation because, at that time, a greater portion of the earth's surface was covered with water.

During the long process of readapting to sea life, porpoises exchanged legs for flippers and grew streamlined, averaging in length between 5 to 12 feet. However, finger bones can still be found in their flippers and they must breathe air through lungs while surfacing. Unlike man, porpoises breathe consciously every six minutes by inhaling two gallons of air within a half-second.

A porpoise's brain is 20 to 40 percent larger than that of man. With that in mind, some scientists believe that in addition to peforming desultory tricks, porpoises probably have the basic capabilities of learning language.

In water, a porpoise communicates by producing sounds originating from air passages in its head. The waterborne sounds move at a speed four times faster than the airborne sounds man is accustomed to. When two porpoises are together, they will exchange a long series of sounds that vary in frequency and length. One remains courteously silent while the other is "talking."

When in the presence of human beings, porpoises politely revert to using mostly airborne sounds that resemble clicks and whistles containing elements of human speech. In fact, porpoises produce humanoid sounds when they hear human speech and come in close contact with people. Aristotle, in 300 B.C., insisted that "the voice of the porpoise in air is like that of a human; that he pronounces vowels and combinations of vowels." A porpoise's initiative deserves praise, considering that few, if any, humans have ever attempted to place their heads in water and attempt waterborne communication.

Some scientists have experimented with creating an interspecies language. An average of 1,000 vocalized syllables, arranged in chains of one to ten sounds, were given to several porpoises. Each animal was rewarded if it correctly repeated the exact series. One porpoise mimicked the vocalizations with few mistakes in either pronunciation or in timing. A human being's memory span limits most people to remembering and repeating chains containing only seven consecutive sounds.

Although concerned scientists seriously study porpoises, other people seriously study profit and have exploited the porpoise's intelligence for both commercial and military use.

The United States Navy, for example, has been attempting to train porpoises to locate underwater objects, such as sunken ships, submarines, or torpedoes by following acoustic signals reflected by the objects. The Navy also trains porpoises to attack sharks that threaten personnel engaged in underwater salvage or rescue work. A porpoise's hard bony snout and high speed acts as an effective battering ram that has earned the respect of sharks.

Commercial enterprises have also exploited the talents of the porpoise. There are more than a dozen aquariums, marinelands, or oceanariums from Florida to California that buy porpoises, then make them earn their keep by jumping through fiery hoops, dancing, raising flags, and playing basketball. In Hawaii, a pair of trainers, who noted that Christmas was only a few weeks away, wanted a porpoise to pull a brightly colored sled mounted on styrofoam runners. Whatever the gimmick, porpoises are successfully used to entice curious tourists to part with millions of dollars each year.

Hollywood and television have also made their bid for a piece of the action. One bottlenose porpoise was trained to play a leading role in a movie entitled "Flipper." The film was later stretched out into a weekly TV series with the same name, using several porpoises for the starring role.

Porpoises have become a box office draw, and Florida supplies the demand. About 190 are captured each year from Florida waters and used to supply 80 percent of the American oceanariums and all of Europe's. A freshly captured porpoise brings between $400 and $800. A 12-foot adult weighing over 700 pounds might add shipping and handling charges of about $1,700. Regulations make it illegal to capture any porpoise less than six feet.

Fortunately, concerned conservationists recently aimed their attention on limiting the number of captures. Recently, one marine organization netted ten porpoises off the coasts of Naples and Marco Islands in Florida to be sold to exhibits. Though a permit had been issued by the Florida Department of Natural Resources allowing the organization to capture 22, several protests were made by local residents.

The group insisted that 22 porpoises was a significant number when caught in a limited area. The protests were brought to the attention of the county commissioner who called the captures "crass commercialism." He has been attempting to set a trend in the right direction by asking for an ordinance forbidding the transporting of porpoises "in any manner" from his county.

The Japanese have usually been portrayed as the major killers of porpoises because they use them for food. Between 11,000 and 16,000 are caught for this purpose each year, according to the Japanese government fishing agency. A porpoise is individually valued at about $20 in Japan with variations in price depending upon the annual catch.

Despite international complaints about using porpoises as a food source, the Japanese continue their fishing and defend themselves by pointing an accusing finger at the American tuna industry.

United States tuna fishermen operating out of the West Coast catch up to 45,000 tons of tuna each year. However, because tuna are often inseparable traveling companions with porpoises in Pacific waters, and both feed on similar small fish, porpoises are inadvertently netted, too. In the process, as many as 250,000 porpoises are consciously killed in a year, in addition to those killed by the French, Spanish, and Scandinavian fishing industries.

In 1971 a Congressional subcommittee conducted hearings on proposed legislation designed to stop the useless slaughter of aquatic mammals. Environmentalists insisted that one porpoise death might be too many because so little is known about the size and composition of the porpoise population, or whether those accidental deaths threaten the existence of the species.

As a compromise between environmentalists and commercial fishermen, California representatives introduced a bill that would allow the killing of ocean mammals "if the harrassment, hunting, capturing, or killing is incidental to commercial fishing operations."

The 1972 Federal Marine Mammal Protection Act, in addition to forbidding the United States fishermen from deliberately killing porpoises, also demands that no marine mammal may be taken or imported by any United States citizen or organization or by any person in United States waters.

The law is of little comfort to the porpoise because it provides the United States tuna industry with a loophole that still allows them to kill porpoises "accidentally" or "incidentally," and, in addition, keeps fishermen from reverting back to their older method of pole and line fishing that was effectively used in the early '60s.

The plight of porpoises proves once again that technology in the hands of man becomes a tool used for conquering nature, instead of helping man live with it. As a result, another species becomes threatened with needless extinction because of man's bottomless greed and perverted sense of entertainment. If a porpoise's intelligence is what it is reputed to be, then they will soon discover who their real enemies are. And what will happen then?

Starting Time		Finishing Time	
Reading Time		Reading Rate	
Comprehension		Vocabulary	

Comprehension— Read the following questions and statements. For each one, put an *x* in the box before the option that contains the most complete or accurate answer. Check your answers in the Answer Key on page 108.

1. Compared to the human brain, the porpoise's brain is
   ☐ a. larger.
   ☐ b. smaller.
   ☐ c. superior.
   ☐ d. equal.

2. The origin of the porpoise is
   ☐ a. explained by the theory of evolution.
   ☐ b. lost in a cloak of mystery.
   ☐ c. explained by Greek mythology.
   ☐ d. strange beyond belief.

3. Fishermen captured tuna with pole and line fishing
   - ☐ a. before they switched to nets.
   - ☐ b. until the Federal Marine Mammal Protection Act was signed.
   - ☐ c. after the Federal Marine Mammal Protection Act was signed.
   - ☐ d. during the 1971 Congressional subcommittee hearings.

4. The present plight of the world's porpoise population results from
   - ☐ a. Japanese fishing techniques.
   - ☐ b. public indifference.
   - ☐ c. the Hollywood film industry.
   - ☐ d. human greed.

5. Based on the information supplied in the selection, the greatest threat to the porpoise comes from the
   - ☐ a. fishing industry.
   - ☐ b. entertainment world.
   - ☐ c. military establishment.
   - ☐ d. scientific community.

6. Given the long history of the porpoise's helpfulness to man, man's current treatment of the porpoise
   - ☐ a. is a natural outcome.
   - ☐ b. repays old debts.
   - ☐ c. is dishonorable.
   - ☐ d. is expected.

7. Sharks have a highly developed sense of
   - ☐ a. sight.
   - ☐ c. taste.
   - ☐ b. hearing.
   - ☐ d. smell.

8. The attitude of the author toward the commercial exploitation of porpoises is
   - ☐ a. understanding.
   - ☐ c. impartial.
   - ☐ b. critical.
   - ☐ d. financial.

9. After her ordeal at sea, Yvonne Vladislavich became
   - ☐ a. hostile toward porpoises.
   - ☐ b. grateful toward porpoises.
   - ☐ c. suspicious of porpoises.
   - ☐ d. frightened by porpoises.

10. The final two sentences
    - ☐ a. provide a lighthearted ending to the selection.
    - ☐ b. suggest a solution to the plight of the porpoises.
    - ☐ c. serve as a warning to humans.
    - ☐ d. are designed to shock the reader.

Comprehension Skills

1. recalling specific facts	6. making a judgment
2. retaining concepts	7. making an inference
3. organizing facts	8. recognizing tone
4. understanding the main idea	9. understanding characters
5. drawing a conclusion	10. appreciation of literary forms

Study Skills, Part One—Following is a passage with blanks where words have been omitted. Next to the passage are groups of five words, one group for each blank. Complete the passage by selecting the correct word for each of the blanks.

Reviewing for Examinations, III

2. Develop a New Approach. This can be a technique of real value to you. Rehashing the same old stuff is not very exciting and certainly nothing to look forward to. Try approaching the subject differently; get a ___(1)___ outlook on the material.

For example, put yourself in the role of ___(2)___. Imagine that next semester you will be teaching this subject and you want to review it now so you'll know it well enough to teach.

For biology, take the point of view of a doctor. What does science mean to him? How can he use it in his practice?

Use your imagination. Be both quizmaster and ___(3)___. Ask yourself questions aloud, and answer them aloud for a "prize" of a million dollars and a free trip to Tahiti.

However you do it, adopt a fresh point of view and make the material you are studying come alive.

(1)	rehearsed		methodical
	popular	fresh	familiar
(2)		instructor	writer
	editor	student	chairman
(3)		companion	contestant
	assistant	consumer	enemy

3. Outline the Course. This may appear to be an enormous task to undertake at the end of the semester, but it need not be. Keep your outline ___(4)___ ; do not exceed three pages. The thinking that goes into outlining makes for excellent reviewing.

When you have completed your outline, you will have a picture of your knowledge of the subject. Your ___(5)___ assignment is now organized for you. Each night attack a new part of the outline and fill in the gaps.

Actually, this technique combines two steps in one. When outlining the matter, you are forced to deal with principles and ___(6)___ . All of your study should be to this end: an understanding and retention of main points and principles.

You know from your own experience that you cannot recall everything about a subject. You must become ___(7)___ and choose only the most important elements of the subject. As you do this, you'll be pleased to observe how the recall of major points triggers the recall of accompanying details. You'll find yourself remembering much more than you had originally thought possible.

(4)		
organized		routine
definite	simple	brief

(5)		
oral		written
study	verbal	essay

(6)		
institutions		organizations
generalizations	effects	specifics

(7)		
general		effective
professional	selective	confident

Study Skills, Part Two—Read the study skills passage again, paying special attention to the lesson being taught. Then, without looking back at the passage, complete each sentence below by writing in the missing word or words. Check the Answer Key on page 108 for the answers to Study Skills, Part One, and Study Skills, Part Two.

1. Using a new _____ is a valuable reviewing technique.

2. Use your _____ and adopt a fresh point of view.

3. It is important to make a brief _____ of the course when you study.

4. All your study should be aimed at understanding and retaining the _____ points.

5. Recall only the important _____ of a subject.

16 Organic Gardening in Perspective

by Dr. Milton Salomon

Vocabulary—The five words below are from the story you are about to read. Study the words and their meanings. Then complete the ten sentences that follow, using one of the five words to fill in the blank in each sentence. Mark your answer by writing the letter of the word on the line before the sentence. Check your answers in the Answer Key on page 108.

A. adherents: supporters

B. deleterious: harmful

C. augment: increase

D. inherent: contained within; intrinsic

E. voracious: ravenous; insatiable

_____ 1. The pesticide dieldrin is _____ to fish.

_____ 2. Many young people are _____ of the back-to-nature movement.

_____ 3. There is no _____ danger in man's use of chemical fertilizers.

_____ 4. Some people have a _____ appetite for certain foods.

_____ 5. Plants have an _____ ability to recycle minerals.

_____ 6. _____ to the principles of organic gardening do not use pesticides.

_____ 7. Inspections by the Food and Drug Administration _____ quality-control efforts by growers.

_____ 8. Some people develop a _____ interest in Eastern religion.

_____ 9. Organic gardeners believe that nonorganic compounds have a _____ effect on plants and animals.

_____ 10. Some people turn to communal living to _____ their feeling of unity with nature.

It has only been about a century since the introduction of commercial chemical fertilizers. Since that time, they have become the major source of plant food. Previously, the maintenance of soil fertility depended on the use of animal manures, composts, and crop rotation.

Organic matter has many values, but it has no special health magic.

This does not mean that chemical fertilizers are better than applications of manures, but rather they have become a recognized and tested means of filling new and special demands upon the land. This need was associated with expanding populations, an industrial revolution, and an amazing growth of cities.

The values of organic matter have not decreased, but its major values are for quite different reasons than many organic gardeners believe.

Through the years, there has emerged an understandable yet almost mystical devotion to the idea that only by a system of natural organic, nonchemical, or biodynamic farming would it be possible to maintain a bountiful, healthy agriculture. Traditionally, the adherents of this concept have been a rather small group, mainly middle-aged, who honestly thought this was the only route to take.

Recently, however, the idea has caught the imagination of a broad segment of the youth culture. Generally this group consists of well educated, affluent, middle-class children whose experiences and backgrounds are found in the cities and suburbs. They are a rather unusual segment of the population and no one denies they have made an impact upon our attitudes and values. Their interest in agriculture from a special viewpoint is well worth looking at.

One of the most fascinating by-products of the search by the young for a new identity and meaning in life has been a growing awareness and sensitivity to the natural world and a spiritual awakening of the deeper senses. Evidence of this may be found in a strong yearning for the land, a return to simple values and communal living, a questioning of the establishment, and a revolt against the dehumanizing effects of massive technology. The commitment in many runs very deep and is often accompanied by turning inward, self-denial, asceticism, and, in the extreme, to practices of ancient religious forms associated with the East.

Outwardly, there has evolved a new life-style in dress and manners. More complete involvement often includes a desire for special natural foods and diets. Natural, organic, "macrobiotic," and other health-food stores and outlets that cater to these tastes have mushroomed across the country. Briefly, it is generally accepted by their customers that foods produced and marketed without the use of chemicals (fertilizers, pesticides, additives) are

superior to those grown by modern farm-management practices. Crops grown solely by use of animal manures, composts, and such natural untreated products as ground limestone and rock are believed to be healthier, taste better, and have greater nutritive and life-giving properties.

It is generally accepted by these people that agricultural chemicals are poisonous and deleterious to health and should be avoided. In a broad sense, adherents to this idea are commited to a system of organic or "biodynamic" gardening rather than the commonly recommended practices of modern mechanized argiculture, which includes the use of chemicals. There is much appeal to this concept and many young people (and old) have flocked to the practice and have accepted the whole picture without carefully analyzing some of the claims and accusations.

There is little question that the careless use of pesticides and injudicious additions of certain food preservatives can produce toxic effects in animals and humans. As examples, dieldrin, a pesticide, can cause death in fish, and excess amounts of sodium nitrate, a food additive, can be toxic to very young children.

But government agencies such as the Food and Drug Administration and others continually monitor food products shipped to markets. Allowable residues of chemicals, which are set by law at very low and nontoxic levels, are carefully checked and when there is any doubt about their safety they are withdrawn from sale. The record in this respect, considering the huge quantity and variety of foods reaching the consumer, is very good.

Certainly there must be continuing vigilance in seeing that chemicals used in the production, processing, and preserving of foods have no long- or short-term ill effects on the health of the consumer. However, there is little doubt these chemicals have been most useful in assuring and maintaining high-quality foods in this country.

I believe it important that organic gardeners and special natural-diet advocates distinguish between pesticides, food additives, chemical fertilizers, and organic matter. Their composition, method of application, reasons for usage, and fate in the environment are not the same.

In most instances, pesticides are synthetic chemical compounds not found naturally in the environment. They are used to kill or discourage insects, disease, and weeds. Food additives are normally simpler materials, many occur naturally and are used as preservatives, emulsifiers, coloring agents, and so on. Both pesticides and additives are usually added directly to the plant, animal, or food and may or may not remain as residues on the product. They may or may not be toxic.

The more intriguing story emerges when we compare

organic materials with chemical fertilizers and analyze their role and place in the growth of plants and their effects upon the soil and food. When man discovered that he could use inorganic, mineral fertilizers to substitute and augment organic manures, he was merely imitating nature.

When organic matter breaks down in the soil, mineral fertilizer elements such as nitrates, phosphates, calcium, and others are released to the soil solution for subsequent uptake by plants. When chemical fertilizers are added to soils, the same elements are made soluble rather quickly and they, too, are then absorbed by plant roots. The plant does not and cannot distinguish, for example, nitrate from a compost pile from that coming from an inorganic chemical source. They are the same chemical and once in the plant enter into the life activity with no "memory" or special distinguishing attributes.

The plant plays the near-miraculous role of coordinating the processes of mineral uptake with photosynthesis to form its own organic matter. And it is precisely that organic matter, that is, food, which finds its way back to manure piles, compost heaps, or the supermarket to be reused again in the release of chemical mineral elements to the soil or directly to man. This is the greatest recycling operation of all. I see nothing magical, special, or healthier in foods grown only with organic fertilizers.

There are, however, a number of compelling reasons why we should use as much organic materials as we reasonably and economically can. Certainly, they should not be wasted. Many benefits are derived from manure and composts that cannot be duplicated by chemical fertilizers alone.

Manure and composts store and slowly release nutrients and minor elements to the soil solution; they affect the release of nutrients from inorganic fertilizer sources; they are a source of energy and nutrients for soil organisms; they encourage good soil structure and water movement; they help conserve moisture; they assist the exchange of nutrients from soil colloids, such as clay, to soil solution for plant absorption; they increase carbon dioxide content of the soil; and some manures and composts have inherent growth regulating and antibiotic effects on living things.

On the other hand, there have been fears that continuous use of chemical fertilizers deteriorates the soil, is poisonous to plants and domestic animals, and may result in inferior, poor quality foods. These claims are not supported by careful experimentation and observation performed over the last century. Overwhelming evidence is to the contrary.

Perhaps we should look upon the use of fertilizers as a device created by man to assist nature. Remember that agriculture is for man's purpose and is in effect a diversion and disruption of the balance in nature. When one considers that the practice of agriculture has gone on for several thousand years, the record of the farmer as an environmentalist has not been too bad, relative to some other industries.

We should not forget that man and domestic animals are voracious users and converters of organic compounds into energy. In this sense, they may seriously interrupt the normal organic cycle. The loss of nutrients, for example, through city sewage and garbage disposal, can only partially be reclaimed and this only by the expenditure of great effort and resources, let alone commitment.

It makes very good sense to reuse as much of our waste products as possible. This is a problem that must be faced now. However, based on my experience, I do not believe that for the foreseeable future we can generate and reclaim enough organic residues to be delivered at the right places, at the right time, and in the right condition to feed even our present size and distribution of population.

Additions of chemical fertilizers complement in a very flexible and economical way the benefits derived from organic matter. Chemical fertilizers are a safe, logical way of building and maintaining our soils and agriculture.

Starting Time			*Finishing Time*	
Reading Time			*Reading Rate*	
Comprehension			*Vocabulary*	

Comprehension
— Read the following questions and statements. For each one, put an *x* in the box before the option that contains the most complete or accurate answer. Check your answers in the Answer Key on page 108.

1. When integrated into the soil, organic matter releases
   □ a. emulsifiers.
   □ b. nitrates.
   □ c. soil colloids.
   □ d. pesticides.

2. Chemical fertilizers were introduced on the commercial market to
   □ a. meet the needs of the times.
   □ b. replace organic matter.
   □ c. protect the health of the nation.
   □ d. increase the nutritional value of food.

3. People who patronize health-food stores do so under the assumption that
   - ☐ a. organically grown food is unhealthy.
   - ☐ b. natural foods have life-giving properties.
   - ☐ c. health foods cost less.
   - ☐ d. chemically grown food is sanitary.

4. The author
   - ☐ a. laments the abuses of agriculture.
   - ☐ b. is preoccupied with public apathy.
   - ☐ c. is sympathetic to big business.
   - ☐ d. defends the use of chemical fertilizers.

5. Biodynamic farming
   - ☐ a. contributes to better health.
   - ☐ b. does not contaminate the soil.
   - ☐ c. offers many benefits.
   - ☐ d. none of the above

6. People who condemn chemical fertilizers as dangerous are
   - ☐ a. scientists.
   - ☐ b. alarmists.
   - ☐ c. activists.
   - ☐ d. spiritual saviors.

7. Chemical fertilizers are
   - ☐ a. safer than organic fertilizers.
   - ☐ b. less safe than pesticides.
   - ☐ c. as safe as food additives.
   - ☐ d. safer than either pesticides or additives.

8. This selection ends on a note of
   - ☐ a. regret.
   - ☐ b. reassurance.
   - ☐ c. irony.
   - ☐ d. condemnation.

9. Proponents of biodynamic farming are
   - ☐ a. naive.
   - ☐ b. sincere.
   - ☐ c. callous.
   - ☐ d. disingenuous.

10. The selection attempts to present
   - ☐ a. a biased argument.
   - ☐ b. an undocumented theory.
   - ☐ c. an alarming idea.
   - ☐ d. a balanced viewpoint.

Comprehension Skills

1. recalling specific facts	6. making a judgment
2. retaining concepts	7. making an inference
3. organizing facts	8. recognizing tone
4. understanding the main idea	9. understanding characters
5. drawing a conclusion	10. appreciation of literary forms

Study Skills, Part One—Following is a passage with blanks where words have been omitted. Next to the passage are groups of five words, one group for each blank. Complete the passage by selecting the correct word for each of the blanks.

Reviewing for Examinations, IV

4. Know What to Expect. There is a great deal you can learn about an examination ___(1)___ . If you are "exam-wise," you can plan the best way to study and the kinds of answers to prepare.

First, discover the kind of exam to be given. ___(2)___ exams require you to organize and compose your own answers. Objective tests require you to select the best response to multiple choice questions, or to ___(3)___ statements true or false, or to fill in or match items. The best way to study for both types of examinations will be covered in later selections.

Most instructors don't mind discussing upcoming exams in a general way. Others are very specific in advising you what to prepare for. By all means, be in class and be ___(4)___ when a coming exam is being discussed.

It may also be possible to talk to those who have already

(1)	presently		beforehand
	externally	internally	belatedly

(2)		Multiple choice	Essay
	Prepared	Traditional	Contemporary

(3)		label	write
	observe	make	require

(4)		casual	absent
	present	supportive	alert

_(5)_ the course to discover what sort of test the instructor gives. Does he or she look for facts and details? If so, study accordingly. Does he or she look for an understanding of principles? Does he or she expect his students to reason, to apply knowledge to a specific case? The answers to these questions require a _(6)_ kind of study on your part.

Does the instructor have a favorite question? Is there one item that appears again and again on his or her tests? If so, plan your response in advance.

Don't worry yourself or your instructor trying to get advance "tips," but use wisely whatever solid information is _(7)_ available to you to help plan your studying.

(5)	discussed		taken
	composed	taught	advised

(6)	enjoyable		difficult
	suitable	advanced	basic

(7)	illegally		emotionally
	substantially	legitimately	wisely

Study Skills, Part Two

Study Skills, Part Two—Read the study skills passage again, paying special attention to the lesson being taught. Then, without looking back at the passage, complete each sentence below by writing in the missing word or words. Check the Answer Key on page 108 for the answers to Study Skills, Part One, and Study Skills, Part Two.

1. You can learn a lot about an _____ before it is given.

2. Find out if the examination is an essay type or if it is an _____ type.

3. Most _____ will discuss the upcoming examination with you.

4. Talk with students who have taken the _____ before.

5. Use all the _____ available to help you plan your study.

17 Mononucleosis: The Overtreated Disease

by William A. Nolen, M.D.

Vocabulary—The five words below are from the story you are about to read. Study the words and their meanings. Then complete the ten sentences that follow, using one of the five words to fill in the blank in each sentence. Mark your answer by writing the letter of the word on the line before the sentence. Check your answers in the Answer Key on page 108.

A. contagious: transmissible by contact

B. erroneous: mistaken; inaccurate

C. incriminating: implicating; suggesting involvement in a wrongful act

D. invariably: always; consistently

E. taxing: burdensome

_____ 1. Although mononucleosis is _____ , it is only mildly so.

_____ 2. People hold many _____ beliefs about mononucleosis.

_____ 3. Some doctors _____ overtreat patients with mononucleosis.

_____ 4. Mononucleosis does not _____ lead to enlargement of the spleen.

_____ 5. Some college students find their problems extremely _____ .

_____ 6. The link between the Epstein-Barr virus and mononucleosis is quite _____ .

_____ 7. Treatment of mononucleosis is often based on _____ assumptions about the disease.

_____ 8. Medical experts belive that the Epstein-Barr virus is a _____ virus.

_____ 9. There is _____ evidence that many cases of mononucleosis are overtreated.

_____ 10. People with mononucleosis are often advised to avoid all _____ situations.

At a party I attended recently I overheard a woman telling a group of people about her daughter. "Kathy has mononucleosis," the woman said. "She's going to have to drop out of college for the rest of this semester. Doctor Jones says she'll have to stay home and take it easy until her blood tests are normal, and that may

Infectious mononucleosis is a common disease and only rarely a serious one.

take a couple of months. Meantime, I'm going to have to wash her dishes and silverware separately from the rest of the family's; 'mono' is very contagious."

Her listeners nodded in agreement. Then another woman chipped in with a horror story about how her son, when he came down with mono, had to drop out of college not just for a semester but for an entire year. When a third woman started on *her* mono story, I moved out of hearing range. Who wants to watch a grown man cry?

There is more erroneous information floating around about infectious mononucleosis (or "mono," for short) than about any other disease I know. These misconceptions are the property not only of the lay public but even of some doctors—like Kathy's Dr. Jones—who haven't read an article or listened to a lecture on the disease in 20 years. As a result, hundreds of patients with infectious mononucleosis are being *mis*treated, rather than treated, every year.

Consider Kathy's case. First, she dropped out of school, something that should very seldom be necessary. Second, her doctor ordered her to stay at home and rest till her blood tests were normal—when, in fact, it is the symptoms and not the blood tests that should determine the extent of a patient's activity. Third, Kathy's mother is doing a lot of unnecessary work attempting to protect the rest of the family; in actuality, infectious mononucleosis is not a very contagious disease, and only rarely does more than one case occur in a family at any one time. Kathy is being overtreated for her illness: another victim of "infectious-mono overkill."

Rather than cite a lot of other cases of infectious mononucleosis that have been mistreated, I think it might be best to present the facts, as we know them, about the disease. You can then apply these facts to any cases with which you may be acquainted (and it's a rare person who doesn't know, or hasn't known, a patient with mono) and decide for yourself whether the treatment has been proper.

1. Infectious mononucleosis is almost certainly caused by a virus (the Epstein-Barr virus, if you're interested). I have to say "almost" because the evidence incriminating this virus, although very strong, is circumstantial. However, from the patient's point of view, the only important point to be made here is this: Until we have isolated this virus and proved that it causes infectious mono and *only* infectious mono, it will be impossible to prepare a vaccine to immunize patients against the disease.

2. Ninety-seven percent of infectious-mononucleosis cases occur in patients under 35. Most cases (77 percent) seem to occur between the ages of 12 and 22, and most of these occur in college students. I say "seem to occur" because it's highly likely that infectious mononucleosis occurs frequently in young children in a mild form that goes unrecognized. The apparent peak in the college years may be partly due to the close medical supervision college students usually receive.

3. Infectious mononucleosis is not very contagious. It is popularly known as the "kissing disease," and it's true that you can acquire it by kissing, but not from a brotherly or sisterly peck. There has to be transmission of saliva.

If you're a college student, you might also acquire mono by using your roommate's toothbrush, but you won't catch it simply from breathing the same air. Stories of an entire dormitory's coming down simultaneously with mono are invariably based on unfounded rumors.

4. The usual signs and symptoms of infectious mono are sore throat, fever, swollen glands at the back of the neck, and a general feeling of tiredness. Since these signs and symptoms occur in many other ailments, blood tests must be done to establish that the patient does indeed have mono. One test is a blood smear, which will show—if the patient has mono—that the percentage of lymphocytes in the blood (usually around 20 percent of the total white-blood-cell count) has risen to about 70 percent, and some of the lymphocytes will be abnormal in appearance. Another test, which takes about two minutes, is done by mixing a drop of the patient's blood with a special solution: Clumps will form if the patient has mono. A third test measures the level of the patient's blood's reaction to the mono virus and may serve as a guide to the severity of the infection. This procedure takes about three hours.

5. The treatment of the ordinary case of infectious mononucleosis consists of rest, a wholesome diet, and aspirin for the fever. As a rule, doctors recommend that the patient stay in bed as long as the fever lasts—usually from one to two weeks. After that, the patient can resume routine activities, avoiding overtiredness. Patients who return to their activities early generally get over their weak, tired feeling faster than those who are very cautious about activity. Only rarely should the weakness of infectious mono persist for more than six weeks.

6. Complications can and do occur in some cases. Most of these complications are mild—slight enlargements of the spleen and liver, for example—and require no special treatment.

When the complications are serious (for example,

massive enlargement of the spleen and/or severe involvement of the liver), longer periods of rest may be required. With marked enlargement of the spleen, the patient must be kept quiet and out of active contact sports, which could possibly result in rupture of the spleen. A doctor can determine, usually by physical examination, whether or not the spleen is enlarged.

Sometimes a streptococcus infection of the throat will become superimposed on the infectious-mono inflammation; a doctor can find out whether this has happened by taking a throat culture. If there *is* such a complication, antibiotics should be used to cure the strep infection. But antibiotics have no effect on infectious mononucleosis itself and they should not be used—as some doctors occasionally use them—"prophylactically"; that is, to ward off infections that do not even exist.

For the patient whose throat becomes so sore and swollen that eating and even breathing are difficult, a short course of cortisone therapy may be useful, but only very seldom does this become necessary.

7. Once you have had infectious mono, you become immune to it.

8. If the patient's symptoms—tiredness, depression, general weakness—persist longer than six weeks, it's wise to look for some cause other than infectious mono.

For example, college students who are bored with studying, afraid of examinations, fed up with the whole college scene, will sometimes use a case of mono as an excuse to drop out of the rat race. Whether consciously or unconsciously, they refuse to part with their symptoms until they are able to get out of the taxing situation they are in. Studies have shown that athletes, anxious to get back to their teams, recover from mono much more quickly on the average than do students who have no comparable ambitions. It's a shame—and it happens frequently—to continue to treat a boy or girl for infectious mononucleosis if what is *really* needed is intelligent counseling and advice on how to cope with the stresses of life.

Infectious mono is a common disease and only rarely a serious one. Overtreatment of patients is a far more common cause of disability than is undertreatment. Rest, a balanced diet, aspirin to relieve discomfort, and liberal applications of common sense—this is all the treatment most mononucleosis patients need.

Starting Time		Finishing Time	
Reading Time		Reading Rate	
Comprehension		Vocabulary	

Comprehension— Read the following questions and statements. For each one, put an *x* in the box before the option that contains the most complete or accurate answer. Check your answers in the Answer Key on page 108.

1. Mononucleosis is usually transmitted by
   □ a. physical contact.
   □ b. breathing.
   □ c. saliva.
   □ d. contaminated water.

2. Mononucleosis affects a person's
   □ a. nerves.   □ c. skin.
   □ b. blood.   □ d. liver.

3. Kathy dropped out of school
   □ a. just before the doctor diagnosed her mononucleosis.
   □ b. after the doctor diagnosed her mononucleosis.
   □ c. after missing six weeks of classes.
   □ d. after recovering from her bout with mononucleosis.

4. The purpose of the selection is to
   □ a. criticize the medical profession.
   □ b. encourage further research.
   □ c. reassure victims of mononucleosis.
   □ d. educate the public.

5. The selection supports which of the following conclusions?
   □ a. Doctors should update their knowledge of mononucleosis.
   □ b. Hospitalization is recommended for persons with mononucleosis.
   □ c. Persons with mononucleosis should not frequent public places.
   □ d. Mononucleosis is a rare disease about which little is known.

6. Many doctors need to be
   □ a. assisted in the early detection of mononucleosis.
   □ b. informed about the risk of spleen enlargement.
   □ c. in closer contact with college infirmaries.
   □ d. reeducated about mononucleosis.

7. The presence of mononucleosis can be positively identifed as a result of
   □ a. a short stay in the hospital.
   □ b. consulting the family doctor.
   □ c. observing obvious symptoms.
   □ d. a series of tests.

8. The tone of the last paragraph is
- ☐ a. humorous.
- ☐ b. alarming.
- ☐ c. reassuring.
- ☐ d. melodramatic.

9. Doctors who overtreat mononucleosis do so because they
- ☐ a. fear malpractice suits.
- ☐ b. are concerned for their patient's health.
- ☐ c. make more money that way.
- ☐ d. are not good physicians.

10. The author develops his point of view by means of
- ☐ a. philosophical discussions.
- ☐ b. factual information.
- ☐ c. scientific theories.
- ☐ d. alarming examples.

Comprehension Skills

1. recalling specific facts	6. making a judgment
2. retaining concepts	7. making an inference
3. organizing facts	8. recognizing tone
4. understanding the main idea	9. understanding characters
5. drawing a conclusion	10. appreciation of literary forms

Study Skills, Part One—Following is a passage with blanks where words have been omitted. Next to the passage are groups of five words, one group for each blank. Complete the passage by selecting the correct word for each of the blanks.

Reviewing for Examinations, V

5. Study Quizzes. Study the other tests and quizzes you have taken during the term. Some of the same questions, or variations of them, might be asked again.

All teachers stress what they consider important on quizzes during the term. Reviewing past __(1)__ will assure that you will be covering many of the most important topics in the course.

6. Review Class Questions. Like the rest of us, teachers are creatures of habit. They tend to __(2)__ themselves. During the term, make notes on the questions your instructor asked in class. You can feel confident that questions like these will appear __(3)__ .

Be sure to copy down accurately everything mentioned by the instructor in the pre-exam review. Many lecturers devote their final class to summarizing the course. Questions asked at this time are particularly __(4)__ because the instructor is speaking with the exam in mind.

7. Cram. Devote the final night to cramming. Spend your last moments in an __(5)__ review of all the major facts, principles, and generalizations. Do not be concerned with details at this time; they'll come back to you later.

Cover the items on your outline fully. Be sure that you can define, explain, or describe what is important or essential to each __(6)__ point.

8. Be Ready. Do not stay up too late the night before. Staying up may create worry and anxiety—just the situation you want to avoid in the morning.

On the day of the exam, get up early and have breakfast. Even if it is not your custom to eat, have something. Nervousness can bring on distracting hunger pangs.

Have confidence in your ability. Follow the procedures suggested here, and you'll give a good performance. The best cure for exam jitters is __(7)__ .

(1)	tests	assignments
	lectures	reports courses

(2)	dislike	repeat
	admire criticize	enrich

(3)	again	seriously
	rarely graphically	seldom

(4)	boring	vague
	significant profound	puzzling

(5)	scattered	casual
	quick intensive	needed

(6)	minor	major
	new repeated	familiar

(7)	orientation	celebration
	preparation separation	instruction

Study Skills, Part Two—Read the study skills passage again, paying special attention to the lesson being taught. Then, without looking back at the passage, complete each sentence below by writing in the missing word or words. Check the Answer Key on page 108 for the answers to Study Skills, Part One, and Study Skills, Part Two.

1. Some _____ from old examinations may be asked again.

2. Questions asked by the professor in _____ will probably appear on the test.

3. The instructor speaks at his pre-exam _____ with the test in mind.

4. An intensive review of all major facts is called _____ .

5. Adequate preparation results in good _____ by the students.

18 Dying, One Day at a Time, I

by Robert Lionel

Vocabulary—The five words below are from the story you are about to read. Study the words and their meanings. Then complete the ten sentences that follow, using one of the five words to fill in the blank in each sentence. Mark your answer by writing the letter of the word on the line before the sentence. Check your answers in the Answer Key on page 108.

A. transgressions: crimes; offenses

B. stagnate: fail to progress; vegetate

C. commensurate: equal to; proportional

D. tenet: belief; principle

E. compunction: guilt; misgivings

_____ 1. Most habitual criminals have no _____ about breaking the law.

_____ 2. Aristotle believed that a good judge tried to find a punishment _____ with the crime.

_____ 3. Society pays a big price when it allows a criminal to _____ in jail for years.

_____ 4. The attitude in our society towards ex-convicts pushes many of them to commit new _____ .

_____ 5. While they _____ in jail, most prisoners become increasingly bitter toward society.

_____ 6. Our society holds to the _____ that criminals should be punished for their crimes.

_____ 7. As a result of their _____ , over 500,000 people are now behind bars.

_____ 8. Some people feel no _____ about advocating public execution for skyjackers.

_____ 9. Many ex-convicts cannot find employment _____ with their skills.

_____ 10. In Biblical times, people accepted the _____ that punishment should be sure, swift, and personal.

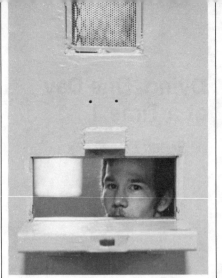

In our contemporary "free" society, there are today in American prisons and correctional institutions more than 500,000 people to whom the concept of "freedom" is a hollow mockery. They have been stored away by their peers for transgressions against the open society; they have forfeited, for a time, their birthright to pursue their individual happiness under an aura of liberty. Many of these men and women, classified as felons, are biding away years of their lives in institutions designated as penitentiaries. The archaic assumption is that time thus spent will result in their becoming "penitent." There is little supportive evidence that anything like that desired self-assessment ever truly takes place. Most emerge, at the end of their sentences, not with an internalized new strength toward self-redirection to better goals—but with a festering bitterness that now it is society who owes *them* a debt! Attempts to collect on that debt, among a society in which they are now twice-watched, contributes to the failure (or recidivist) statistics which prove that nearly two out of every three ex-convicts will return to prison! It is perhaps remarkable that the one out of three manages to stay out, considering the occupational barriers we construct against reintegration into our midst with respectable, competitively paying jobs.

A society which allows half-a-million souls to stagnate behind bars can never call itself wholly "free." To do so makes an obscenity of the word.

The Cost In Souls and Dollars

The half-a-million convicts mentioned at the start of this article pass their tedious days in more than 200 federal and state prisons dotting this land like so many eyeless silos of despair. Together, their sentences comprise more than three million years—ten times longer than man himself has occupied the earth. Today, approximately 5,000 new convicts are incarcerated each year.

The cost to society to maintain the system runs to more than a billion dollars a year. New correctional facilities alone require annual expenditures in excess of $45 million. In one year we spent over $800 million to sustain our prison populations. This averaged out to $2,000 for each felon, $1,000 for each misdemeanant, and $3,600 for each juvenile delinquent, the latter figure being higher based on the theory that we should spend more in an effort to rehabilitate our youthful offenders. Additionally, taxpayers forked over another $196 million to cover the costs of parole for 850,000 ex-convicts.

But what about the inmates themselves? Has all this coin purchased us a "better" convict, a greater respect for society? Not if we believe the statistics just cited on recidivism—that two out of three return to life in the Big House.

As we will see in this article, money unto itself is not the answer to our penal woes. Only the commitment of a society which truly believes that a life is worth saving—

worth "rehabilitating"—can spell the difference between a man or woman making it on the outside, or returning quickly to prison.

Our thinking *must* change. We must realize that a society which allows half-a-million souls to stagnate behind bars can never call itself wholly "free." To do so makes an obscenity of the word.

We do not advocate that all prisons be abolished, but we do advocate that once a man has "paid his debt to society," his time of punishment must end. The man must have a true chance to prove himself, or else we must build bigger prisons from which only death can serve as the ultimate rehabilitation. We must become a *part* of rehabilitation, or a part of the imprisonment. We cannot have it both ways. We cannot release a man and then say to him, "You are yet a criminal in our eyes, and we expect the worst of you. Do not disappoint us." Instead we must say, "We will watch you closely for a while because we know your past, but we will help you to a full, lasting life if that is now your true goal." A man must first be taken at his word—and then his deed. If his words are those of honesty, then we must provide him with the opportunities to turn those words into deeds. We will know his genuine intent soon enough.

I do not believe that most ex-convicts want to return to a life of crime immediately upon release. They want a job commensurate with their pre-criminal abilities. They want the love of a family, the warmth of a woman. They want to feel the starch in a fresh shirt, the privacy of a bathroom, the pleasures of a bedroom. In short, they want all those things—more desperately than we can ever imagine—which were denied them so long.

But what do they find? Hostility. Suspicion. Fear. But, most horrible of all, they find apathy. They emerge from prison shedding the walled cocoon of their incarcerated lives only to find higher walls of public scorn and disinterest. Soon, they give up. They then go to those people who will not stare at them, nor run from them babbling syrupy platitudes. They go to their most recent friends—the friends they made in prison. And from those meetings, it is a one-way street back to the cement courtyards.

We can blame a man when he commits a crime—and we can fit a punishment to suit that crime. But we cannot blame a man when he comes out. If he fails during those first few days, or weeks, or months, the blame most usually falls upon us all, we free men of the free society. We who carry the theory of equal opportunity within our troubled consciences like so many pennies in a rich man's suit. We of the American Dream.

The Theory of Rehabilitation

A tenet of rehabilitation of the alcoholic begins with

self-acknowledgment that one *has the problem.* Only then can help have a chance for success. Can this rubric not be extended to apply to the felon? Until he can accept the immorality of his act, there is little room to move him toward an internalized and subjective goal of redirected, socially constructive, positive behavior.

If an ex-convict perceives that society will never help him, be assured he will feel little compunction, and few uneasy twinges, when the opportunity to offend that society again presents itself. Our help should not spring from this fear, but from the highest philosophic or religious ethics our reason and civilization have developed—those traits which have hopefully set us above the other animals.

Present-day criminologists, average men, and thinkers and philosphers centuries before Christ have agonized about the management of those who offend and assault and prey upon their contemporary societies—yet few writers have undertaken to bring these ideas together for examination.

In 1748 the great French philosopher Rousseau made the observation that "frequent punishments are always a sign of weaknesses or remissness on the part of government." On the point of rehabilitation, he observed "there is not a single ill-doer who could not be turned to some good." On capital punishment, his comment was to the effect that the state "has no right to put to death, even for the sake of making an example, anyone whom it can leave alive without danger." On the subject of pardon, or exempting the guilty from a penalty imposed by the law and pronounced by the judge, he felt that this right belongs "only to an authority which is superior to both judge and law." This he defined as the sovereign. In a well-governed state, he observed there are few punishments. Not because there are many pardons, but because criminals are rare. It is when a state is in decay, so Rousseau believed, that the multitude of crime grows out of proportion.

As early as 334 B.C., in his *Nicomacheon Ethics,* Aristotle observed that "man commits unjust actions voluntarily and, by taking the initiative, reveals that he acted by his own choice." He went on to say, "This injustice amounts to an inequality which the judge tries to equalize—by means of the penalty, the judge takes away from the gain of the offender." By gain he meant not only gains such as by stealing, but he extended this even to the inflicting of a wound. The wound is a "loss" to the sufferer even though there has been no real "gain" to the criminal. Moreover, in his essay on politics written about the same time, Aristotle conceptualized the need for the separation of the duties of judges and jailors. He saw the judicial process as odious at best, but "a double odium is incurred when the judges who have passed also executed the sentence, and if they are also the executioners, they will be the enemies of all." In a lecture to the people of Athens, he spoke of the separate functions of a jailor, and wondered if some device could not be arrived at to render the office less unpopular. He felt jailors are "as necessary as executioners, but good men do all they can to avoid either position." He felt worthless persons could not be safely trusted with being jailors, for "many themselves require a guard, and are not fit to guard others."

In Biblical times, justice apparently was swift and personal and final. It may be we have come full circle and justice and punishment are being once again seen as one and the same, and the element of personal vengeance cannot be separated out. Indeed, a frightened populace and its media may be in concert to form a symbiotic relationship with a demand that an impersonal crime be punished personally and publicly, as witness the many recent suggestions offered as suitable punishment for skyjackers, not the least of which is public execution.

Starting Time		Finishing Time	
Reading Time		Reading Rate	
Comprehension		Vocabulary	

Comprehension
— Read the following questions and statements. For each one, put an *x* in the box before the option that contains the most complete or accurate answer. Check your answers in the Answer Key on page 108.

1. Parole programs for ex-convicts cost taxpayers about
   ☐ a. $850 thousand per year.
   ☐ b. $45 million per year.
   ☐ c. $196 million per year.
   ☐ d. $1 billion per year.

2. In the opening paragraph, the author supports which of the following statements?
   ☐ a. Society should keep a closer watch on ex-convicts.
   ☐ b. Prisoners should not be denied their right to freedom and happiness.
   ☐ c. In general, prisoners have a poor record of rehabilitation.
   ☐ d. The judicial system is responsible for bitterness felt by ex-convicts.

3. Many ex-convicts return to crime
   - ☐ a. even before they meet their parole officer.
   - ☐ b. only after coming into contact with other ex-convicts.
   - ☐ c. after realizing how profitable it can be.
   - ☐ d. after finding themselves scorned by society.

4. The author is a firm believer that recidivism can be reduced if
   - ☐ a. ex-convicts cooperate with society.
   - ☐ b. society undergoes a change of attitude.
   - ☐ c. prison conditions are made less attractive.
   - ☐ d. society agrees to spend more money.

5. Which of the following conclusions can be drawn from the selection?
   - ☐ a. Juvenile delinquents should not be given special treatment.
   - ☐ b. The American public is sensitive to the plight of ex-convicts.
   - ☐ c. Human nature is constant and will never change.
   - ☐ d. This free society must reconsider its attitudes toward prisons.

6. The author's attitude toward rehabilitation is
   - ☐ a. positive.
   - ☐ b. unrealistic.
   - ☐ c. negative.
   - ☐ d. dangerous.

7. Justice and punishment should be
   - ☐ a. personal and final.
   - ☐ b. kept separate.
   - ☐ c. administered swiftly.
   - ☐ d. slow and deliberate.

8. The author's attitude toward recidivists is
   - ☐ a. harsh.
   - ☐ b. sympathetic.
   - ☐ c. friendly.
   - ☐ d. humorous.

9. After release from prison, ex-convicts quickly become
   - ☐ a. lonely and disillusioned.
   - ☐ b. sad and frightened.
   - ☐ c. arrogant and boastful.
   - ☐ d. happy and carefree.

10. The expression ". . . like so many eyeless silos of despair" is an example of
    - ☐ a. a personification.
    - ☐ b. a simile.
    - ☐ c. a metaphor.
    - ☐ d. an alliteration.

Comprehension Skills

1. recalling specific facts	6. making a judgment
2. retaining concepts	7. making an inference
3. organizing facts	8. recognizing tone
4. understanding the main idea	9. understanding characters
5. drawing a conclusion	10. appreciation of literary forms

Study Skills, Part One—Following is a passage with blanks where words have been omitted. Next to the passage are groups of five words, one group for each blank. Complete the passage by selecting the correct word for each of the blanks.

Taking Objective Exams

Objective-type examinations consist of multiple choice, matching, fill-in, and ___(1)___ type questions. Answering questions on objective examinations will produce better results if you follow these rules and steps.

Rule 1. Answer all of the questions. Even when you are penalized for wrong answers, your chances of scoring higher are better if you ___(2)___ a hunch rather than leave the question unanswered.

Rule 2. Do not change an answer unless you know for sure that it is incorrect. Sometimes, a later question may reveal that one of your earlier responses was ___(3)___. Otherwise, go with your first choice.

Rule 3. Use all of the time. Do not be tempted to finish early. Give yourself every ___(4)___. Take every bit of the time scheduled for the examination.

Keeping these three rules in mind, follow these procedures when you answer the questions.

(1)	familiar	similar	
	varied	other	some
(2)	follow	ignore	
	condemn	invent	borrow
(3)	correct	valuable	
	revealing	wrong	worthless
(4)	encouragement	penalty	
	advantage	discipline	luxury

ANSWER EASY QUESTIONS

Divide the examination period into three equal parts. During the first period, read all of the questions. Answer those that are easy and whose answers you know ___(5)___ . If you must stop to think over a response, go on to the next. Doing the easy ones first helps to settle you down. We all tend to be anxious at first, and seeing questions we know the answers to eliminates uncertainty about what to expect. Also, answering the easy ones gets us off to a secure start.

ANSWER LESS DIFFICULT QUESTIONS

During the second period, read all of the unanswered questions. If after a brief pause you can supply an answer, mark it and go on. Follow your hunches now. Mark all of those you ___(6)___ you know. Leave the most difficult blank.

ANSWER DIFFICULT QUESTIONS

During the third round you will have more time to spend answering the ___(7)___ questions. Take your time and choose the best or most likely answer. Answer all the questions this time.

(5)   eagerly   leisurely
     hopefully   immediately   eventually

(6)   know   consider
     doubt   wish   think

(7)   easy   difficult
     interesting   unrelated   sequential

Study Skills, Part Two—Read the study skills passage again, paying special attention to the lesson being taught. Then, without looking back at the passage, complete each sentence below by writing in the missing word or words. Check the Answer Key on page 108 for the answers to Study Skills, Part One, and Study Skills, Part Two.

1. Objective exams consist of _____ , matching, and fill-in questions.

2. Your chances for a high score are better if you answer _____ of the questions.

3. It is wise to use all of the _____ provided and not be tempted to finish early.

4. Divide the time into _____ equal parts.

5. Answer the easiest questions first, leaving the most difficult until _____ .

19 | # Dying, One Day at a Time, II

by Robert Lionel

Vocabulary—The five words below are from the story you are about to read. Study the words and their meanings. Then complete the ten sentences that follow, using one of the five words to fill in the blank in each sentence. Mark your answer by writing the letter of the word on the line before the sentence. Check your answers in the Answer Key on page 108.

A. provision: plans; preparations

B. disrepute: disgrace; disfavor

C. collude: secretly participate in

D. laudable: deserving praise

E. apathy: lack of feeling; indifference

_____ 1. Groups such as the Jaycees have made _____ contributions to the rehabilitation of prisoners.

_____ 2. Over the years, local jails have fallen into _____ .

_____ 3. Correction authorities have recently come up with some _____ new ideas for dealing with criminals.

_____ 4. _____ must be made for prisoners to maintain contact with their families.

_____ 5. It is a shame that the public has shown such _____ toward the plight of ex-convicts.

_____ 6. It is time for our prison system to move away from its current state of _____ .

_____ 7. Disreputable prison officials may _____ in racial or sexual attacks on prisoners.

_____ 8. In dealing with prisoners, halfway houses show none of the _____ displayed by the general public.

_____ 9. Guards have been known to _____ in prison drug deals.

_____ 10. Society has not made proper _____ for dealing with ex-convicts.

The earliest function of jails in Anglo-Saxon society, from which we derive most of our social institutions, was to safely keep accused persons to be sure they were on hand to stand trial when the King's traveling judges came around. This responsibility dates back to the 10th century and it was several centuries later before jails also became places of punishment for petty offenders, vagrants, and debtors.

While punishment is the right of society, rehabilitation is the responsibility of that society.

It is natural that the colonists who came to America set up local jails to serve as British counterparts in the new country. Later, when Quaker humane influence turned the new country against the barbarous forms of corporal punishment that had been inflicted upon more serious offenders, imprisonment for long periods of time became the general practice and a new kind of institution called the penitentiary came into being. Customarily, these facilities have been administered by the states and, later, by the federal government.

The jails, keeping their time-honored functions of detaining accused persons and offenders serving short sentences, remained under local control. At the same time, probably because of their accessibility, they were used to deal with other kinds of problem people, including the insane, children who could not be controlled elsewhere, alcoholics, and men who would not support their families. In short, jails have tended to become convenient repositories for all kinds of misfits for whom society has not made more adequate provision.

Given the limitations of local financing, absence of essential programming, resources, and the impossibly diverse problems heaped upon them, it is little wonder that local jails have been in disrepute for their archaic methods of operation. Many harsh words have been directed toward the jails and the people who run them, but few systematic attempts have been made to correct the sources of their long-standing evils.

Today, there are new trends along the whole range of correctional thinking and practice which forecast the possibility of new and more constructive uses of local jails. These trends must be taken into account in planning new or remodeled local correctional facilities both for these reasons and for the added likelihood that other program developments and procedural changes may well have an effect on the number and kinds of our jail populations.

Rehabilitation: It Can Work

Theoretically, rehabilitation is a primary objective of imprisonment, but in practice it is subordinated to the intended deterrent effects of tight custody, regimentation, and a climate of repression. The "good prisoner" is one who seems subdued in that environment—a serious drawback to successful social adjustment after release. Prison systems range in quality from marginal acceptability in those of a few states and the federal government, down to the medieval level of some state and local systems. Facilities are severely overcrowded and are generally below acceptable physical standards; narcotics traffic and sexual abuses thrive.

The failure rate is very high: 63 percent of federal parolees released in one year were rearrested within six years, as were 76 percent of those given mandatory releases. Such information as is available indicates that experience with state prison releases is comparable. The appalling fact is that firm statistical data on recidivism is practically nonexistent at state and local levels. Only occasional spot studies have been made and coordination of records from the many state, local, and federal institutions has not been attempted.

Rehabilitative efforts vary, but few teachers, psychologists, or psychiatrists are found on prison staffs. Many inmates have no work assignments; idleness is the chief prison occupation. Custodial restraints then breed resentment. The work that is available rarely fosters skills useful after discharge. Experience in producing license plates or mail bags has slight value on the outside labor market.

Every objective study of American prisons has called attention to the low qualifications of prison guards, and to their lack of intensive training. Both the nature of their work and compensation scales are unattractive. The usual disciplinary emphasis encourages brutalization, greatly worsened where guards collude in the drug traffic or overlook inmate violence extending to homosexual assaults. Lives of prisoners are endangered by racial violence and other forms of hostility. In many prisons, moreover, tensions between all-white staffs and prison populations dominated by militant blacks have reached explosive levels. Prisoners usually lack avenues of complaint and are denied access to legal counsel or other protections of due process; they are made to feel subhuman.

Before rehabilitation can be truly effective, a change must come about in the minds of men. Society must realize that building penal facilities is not the only answer. Not all criminals are locked up for life. They serve their sentence and are released. They come back into society more hardened than before. They have had time to think and plan their method by which they can "get even" with the society that put them behind bars.

Not until the offender can "believe in" the society of which he has never before been a part, can genuine rehabilitation work. But first, a "rehabilitation" in thinking must take place within the public at large.

It's Up to Us

We need action. We need a public which admits and understands that jail as punishment is not effective. The concept has failed; vengeance purely and simply dehumanizes both the convicted prisoners and society itself.

We need a public that is willing to accept some of the new ideas which correction authorities are talking about at this time. These are not the wild ideas of "do-gooders." They are the result of years of planning and consideration by concerned penologists, psychologists, and sociologists who have worked out new programs: programs in which the convict leaves prison during the day to work and returns to prison at night; programs of regulated conjugal visits for long-term prisoners so the prisoner, once released, still has a family to go home to, (or don't we believe that families are stabilizing influences and that these men need as much stability as society can give them?) We need programs that include training for skilled jobs; aftercare programs to get a released felon past that crucial first three months of freedom, something to bridge the gap between the closed society of prison and the sudden variety of choices confronting the "free" man; programs that pay for the jobs performed within prisons at a decent pay level so the convict, once released, is not obliged as the first order of business to stick up a store in order to get money to eat.

Law enforcement is everybody's business, not only the police's, but the "correctional" system's as well. The average law-abiding citizen is satisfied to confine the criminal in a maximum security prison far from the community, and this is exactly what we have been doing. It has not worked.

But rehabilitation *does* work. The establishment of halfway houses—places located within the community where ex-convicts can receive counseling and make a gradual reentry into society—demonstrate that ex-convicts so maintained suffer a great deal less recidivism than those convicts released directly from prisons. Additionally, such laudable programs as The United States Jaycees "Protect Re-Con," plus the establishment of in-prison Jaycee chapters, reduce the recidivistic rate tremendously. It has been demonstrated that convicts who become Jaycees while in prison have a return rate after release of only 15 to 20 percent!

The single major problem faced by rehabilitation is the apathy of the general citizenry. We just don't want to get involved. Even concerned social action groups, such as the Jaycees, find it difficult to enlist the wholehearted support of their membership. The groups will tackle willingly such immense problems such as VD, drugs, and alcoholism, but they shy away frequently from active work in criminal rehabilitation programs. Similarly, Congress and state legislatures get very nervous when asked for additional sums to undertake sweeping programs of penal reform. However, thanks, in a very sick way, to such horrors as the Attica riot and the Arkansas prison scandals, hopes are higher now that legislative bodies are becoming more responsive to the conditions of the United States prison system, both on the federal and local level.

While punishment is the *right* of society, rehabilitation is the *responsibility* of that society. No nation can afford to waste the human potential inherent in million of lives. Criminal rehabilitation is the one hope we have in reclaiming a majority of that potential. The stakes are too high to pull out of the game. The time is growing too short to look the other way. We, the citizens, must make a decision: Do we now practice what we preach—that man is noble and life sacred—or do we turn our backs and forever throw the keys of hope down the gutter of despair?

Starting Time		Finishing Time	
Reading Time		Reading Rate	
Comprehension		Vocabulary	

Comprehension
— Read the following questions and statements. For each one, put an *x* in the box before the option that contains the most complete or accurate answer. Check your answers in the Answer Key on page 108.

1. Most of our present-day social institutions are derived from
   - ☐ a. Anglo-Saxon society.
   - ☐ b. the Quaker philosophy.
   - ☐ c. British institutions.
   - ☐ d. the Dark Ages.

2. The development of prisons over the centuries has been
   - ☐ a. humane.
   - ☐ b. necessary and expensive.
   - ☐ c. enlightened.
   - ☐ d. gradual and expanding.

3. Legislatures became more receptive to the idea of prison reforms
   - ☐ a. when the Jaycees began pressuring them.
   - ☐ b. as a result of the high recidivism rate.
   - ☐ c. after the corruption of prison guards was revealed.
   - ☐ d. after the Attica riot and Arkansas prison scandals.

4. American penal institutions
   - ☐ a. require minor improvements.
   - ☐ b. operate at maximum efficiency.
   - ☐ c. reflect society's apathy.
   - ☐ d. conform to basic standards.

5. The author concludes that jails presently contain a variety of misfits because
   - ☐ a. society prefers easy solutions.
   - ☐ b. crime is out of control.
   - ☐ c. doctors are in short supply.
   - ☐ d. society must be protected.

6. The reasons for the current state of penal institutions are
   - ☐ a. oversimplified.
   - ☐ b. complex.
   - ☐ c. questionable.
   - ☐ d. financial.

7. The "good prisoner" is
   - ☐ a. a rehabilitated prisoner.
   - ☐ b. an innocent person.
   - ☐ c. a disadvantaged person.
   - ☐ d. a prison informer.

8. The author's plea for an end to society's apathy is delivered in a
   - ☐ a. strident tone.
   - ☐ b. cajoling tone.
   - ☐ c. self-deprecating tone.
   - ☐ d. hostile tone.

9. For the most part, prisoners are
   - ☐ a. bored and restless.
   - ☐ b. meek and submissive.
   - ☐ c. self-reliant and aloof.
   - ☐ d. cruel and calculating.

10. The selection is written in the form of
   - ☐ a. a debate.
   - ☐ b. a short story.
   - ☐ c. a news report.
   - ☐ d. an exposition.

Comprehension Skills

1. recalling specific facts
2. retaining concepts
3. organizing facts
4. understanding the main idea
5. drawing a conclusion
6. making a judgment
7. making an inference
8. recognizing tone
9. understanding characters
10. appreciation of literary forms

Study Skills, Part One—Following is a passage with blanks where words have been omitted. Next to the passage are groups of five words, one group for each blank. Complete the passage by selecting the correct word for each of the blanks.

Taking Essay Examinations

Following certain rules and using certain techniques when taking examinations can result in higher grades. Procedures that organize and improve your performance permit you to ___(1)___ your knowledge of the subject to the best advantage.

Another type of examination is the essay or composition type. This requires the student to ___(2)___ responses to several questions. Many students dislike this type, preferring objective-type questions. Yet knowing how to handle the written examination produces better results.

OUTLINE ANSWERS

Outline the answers to all questions before doing any writing. ___(3)___ your outline to main headings only. Include a subhead only if you feel you may forget it.

BALANCE OUTLINES

Look over all of your outlines. Some will be complete; others will be weak. Transfer some of the headings from the strong answers to the weak ones. This will give you confidence in answering because you will know something about all of them. The questions are all on the same ___(4)___ so a little deliberation will indicate how you can transfer headings and make them applicable to other questions.

(1)
	forget	create
use	forecast	expand

(2)
	compose	select
reject	list	avoid

(3)
	Expand	Confine
Project	Remove	Transfer

(4)
	opportunity	derivation
basis	subject	location

APPORTION TIME

Divide your time proportionately. Base your time allotments on the (5)____ value of the questions—spend more time on those that are worth more. If all of the questions are of equal value, devote equal time to each answer. This permits you to make your answers of generally similar length, concealing any weaknesses in your answers. A too-short answer signals the instructor that your knowledge on a certain question is (6)____ . Avoid giving such signals.

WRITE LEGIBLY

Even if your answers must be shorter, take the time to make your (7)____ clear and readable.

| (5) | personal | ultimate |
| | face | unseen | credit |

| (6) | lacking | extensive |
| | sufficient | specialized | incorrect |

| (7) | thoughts | facts |
| | handwriting | conclusions | relationships |

Study Skills, Part Two—Read the study skills passage again, paying special attention to the lesson being taught. Then, without looking back at the passage, complete each sentence below by writing in the missing word or words. Check the Answer Key on page 108 for the answers to Study Skills, Part One, and Study Skills, Part Two.

1. Knowing how to handle the _____ exam produces better results.

2. Only the subheads that may be _____ should be included in the outline.

3. Headings in the outline can be _____ from the strong answers to the weak ones.

4. Lack of knowledge on a subject is often indicated by an answer that is too _____ .

5. Good handwriting that is clear and _____ is important in an essay examination.

Vocabulary—The five words below are from the story you are about to read. Study the words and their meanings. Then complete the ten sentences that follow, using one of the five words to fill in the blank in each sentence. Mark your answer by writing the letter of the word on the line before the sentence. Check your answers in the Answer Key on page 108.

A. nil: nothing; zero

B. controversy: dispute

C. insulated: surrounded by protective material

D. potent: powerful

E. meager: scanty; scarce

_____ 1. In the Salton Sea area of California, a _____ amount of steam and water comes to the surface naturally.

_____ 2. The amount of energy currently being harnessed from volcanoes is _____ .

_____ 3. An _____ reservoir of molten magma can be an excellent source of geothermal power.

_____ 4. Active volcanoes discharge _____ bursts of steam.

_____ 5. There is some _____ surrounding the origin of the earth's volcanic belts.

_____ 6. In the first half of the 20th century, there was _____ commercial development of geothermal fields.

_____ 7. The need to find new sources of energy provides a _____ impetus to the development of geothermal power.

_____ 8. Many deep, _____ pockets of hot water or steam have little surface leakage.

_____ 9. Development of geothermal fields may lead to _____ if it involves the destruction of the world's natural geysers.

_____ 10. With geothermal reservoirs, the cost of pumping hot fluid to the surface is _____ .

With increasing population and industrial expansion, domestic requirements for electric power have been doubling about every ten years. To meet these growing needs, government and industry are vigorously investigating and rapidly developing new sources of energy. Among the possible new sources, atomic energy probably has the largest potential, but geothermal energy—a previously little-explored source—may prove to be most important in many areas.

Is natural steam a possible important source of energy for the future?

For years man has viewed with awe the spectacular bursts of natural steam from volcanoes, geysers, and boiling springs. Although the use of hot springs for baths dates to ancient times, the use of natural steam for the manufacture of electric power did not begin until 1905. That year the first geothermal power station was built at Larderello, Italy. For the next several decades, there were no other major developments in the field, and even now Italy leads the world in power production from natural steam. New Zealand began major exploration of hot spring and geyser areas in 1950, and successful results there proved that commercial steam can be developed from areas containing very hot water rather than steam at depth. Today, the United States, Japan, and the Soviet Union are also producing power from geothermal sources, and Iceland uses hot water from geyser fields for space heating. Many other countries have geothermal energy potential, and several are now conducting exploration for sources to be developed.

In the United States, the first commercial geothermal power plant was built by the Pacific Gas and Electric Co., in 1960 at "The Geysers," California.

Sites for Geothermal Exploration

Most of the promising areas for geothermal power development are within belts of volcanic activity. A major belt called "the ring of fire" surrounds the Pacific Ocean. The "hot spots" favorable for geothermal energy are related to volcanic activity in the present and not-too-distant past. In the western United States, particularly along the Pacific Coast, widespread and intense volcanic activity has occurred during the past ten million years. The record of volcanism in our western states, therefore, holds promise for geothermal power development. Currently, exploration for power sites is focused in California, Nevada, Oregon, and New Mexico, with some interest being displayed in the whole region from the Rocky Mountains to the Pacific Ocean.

Sources for Commercial Steam

Volcanoes produce the most dramatic displays of natural steam. Water that comes into contact with molten lava (temperatures of 2,000 degrees Fahrenheit and higher) near the earth's surface can exist only as steam. Rapid expansion of steam and other gases below the surface causes some of nature's most violent and explosive eruptions.

Almost all active volcanoes have fumaroles, or vents, that discharge steam and other hot gases. But, despite the large quantities of steam discharged during active volcanism, the energy cannot be harnessed as a dependable source of power. In some areas the emission of steam cannot be controlled, and in other areas the costs of controlling the steam would exceed the value of the power obtained.

More promising sources for commercial steam are certain other subsurface hot spots or geothermal reservoirs that are generally found in areas of volcanism. These reservations contain larger and more dependable volumes of steam or hot water. Wells are drilled into the reservoirs to tap the naturally hot fluids that may drive power generators.

Most known geothermal reservoirs contain hot water, rather than steam. Water at depth and under high pressure remains liquid at temperatures far above 212 degrees Fahrenheit, the boiling point of water at sea level. When this water is tapped by drilled wells and rises to the surface, the pressure falls. As the pressure decreases, the water boils, perhaps violently, and the resulting steam is separated from the remaining liquid water. Because the well itself acts as a continuously erupting geyser, the expanding steam propels the liquid water to the surface and pumping costs are nil.

Why Do Hot Spots Exist?

Mineral exploration over the world has shown that temperatures in deep mines and oil wells usually rise with increasing depth below the surface. One popular explanation assumes that our planet has a fiery origin and that a shallow crustal layer encases a large molten core. Most geologists, however, now believe that our planet was not hot when it first formed. The weight of the evidence suggests instead that a natural radioactivity, present in small amounts in all rocks, has gradually heated the earth, and that heat is still being produced. Geophysical studies also indicate that the molten core is much smaller than was once supposed, and that it is not, in itself, a source of the heat in the earth's crust. The reasons for the existence and specific location of the earth's volcanic belts are still subjects of vigorous scientific study and controversy, but the energy from natural radioactivity in rocks of the earth's crust and upper mantle is the fundamental cause of heat within the earth.

Types of Geothermal Fields

In a general way, geothermal fields are either hot spring systems or deep insulated reservoirs that have little leakage of heated fluids to the surface. Yellowstone National Park and Wairakei, New Zealand, are examples of large hot spring systems. Larderello in Italy and the Salton Sea area of California are examples of insulated reservoirs.

Hot springs have a plumbing system of interconnected channels within rocks. Water from rain or snow seeps underground. If the water reaches a local region of greater heat it expands and rises, being pushed onward by the pressure from new cold and heavy water that is just entering the system. The hot water is discharged as hot springs or geysers.

Deep reservoirs with little surface area have porous rocks (like those in a petroleum reservoir) capped by rocks such as clays and shales that prevent the free upward escape of water and heat. Larderello, Italy, and the Salton Sea area of California are examples of this type. Both reservoirs have feeble thermal springs coming to the surface, but there may be undiscovered areas that have no leakages.

Hot Water and Dry Steam Systems

Because of the pressures at great depths, water can be entirely liquid rather than steam deep in hot spring and insulated reservoir systems, even at very high temperatures. Steam forms in these systems if the hot water rises to levels where the pressure drops to the point where water can boil. This flashing of steam from liquid water is the major potential source of geothermal energy for commercial use because natural hot water systems are relatively abundant.

However, in a few explored systems the heat supply is so high and the rate of discharge of water is so low that steam forms deep in the system. Larderello in Italy and "The Geysers" in California are examples of the less common reservoirs of dry natural steam.

Characteristics Favorable for Geothermal Reservoirs

The most favorable geologic factors for a geothermal reservoir of commercial value include:
1. A potent source of heat, such as a large chamber of molten magma. The chamber should be deep enough to insure adequate pressure and a slow rate of cooling, and yet not too deep for natural circulation of water and effective transfer of heat to the circulating water.

Magma chambers of this type are most likely to occur in regions of recent volcanism, such as the Rocky Mountain and Pacific states.
2. Large and porous reservoirs with channels connected to the heat source, near which water can circulate and then be stored in the reservoir. Even in areas of slight rainfall, enough water may percolate underground to sustain the reservoir.
3. Capping rocks of low permeability that inhibit the flow of water and heat to the surface. In very favorable circumstances, cap rocks are not essential for a commercial field. However, a deep and well-insulated reservoir is likely to have much more stored energy than an otherwise similar but shallow and uninsulated reservoir.

The Potential of Geothermal Power

It is too early to judge whether natural steam has the potential to satisfy an important part of the world's requirements for electric power, but in locally favorable areas it is already an attractive source for cheap power. Current exploration, based upon geologic and geophysical methods, is likely to develop presently undiscovered fields. The recent discovery of a new field at Monte Amiata, Italy—where there are only meager surface manifestations of abnormal geothermal energy—was based in part on the use of such methods. These are now well enough developed to support exploration for wholly concealed reservoirs.

All natural geyser areas of the world are potential sites for commercial geothermal energy, yet it is to be remembered that development of these areas for the recovery of steam may destroy the geysers themselves. Although the need to develop new sources of energy may become urgent, still every effort must be made to protect these scenic wonders of nature.

Starting Time		Finishing Time	
Reading Time		Reading Rate	
Comprehension		Vocabulary	

Comprehension— Read the following questions and statements. For each one, put an *x* in the box before the option that contains the most complete or accurate answer. Check your answers in the Answer Key on page 108.

1. According to the author, which of the following sources of energy seems to have the greatest potential?
   - ☐ a. atomic power
   - ☐ b. natural steam
   - ☐ c. natural gas
   - ☐ d. oil shale

2. The increasing demands for power are related to
   - ☐ a. decreasing world supplies.
   - ☐ b. people and their needs.
   - ☐ c. new scientific exploration.
   - ☐ d. wasteful use of energy.

3. The natural radioactivity in rocks
 - ☐ a. caused the earth's molten core to shrink.
 - ☐ b. was caused by the earth's molten core.
 - ☐ c. resulted in the gradual heating of the earth.
 - ☐ d. resulted in volcanic belts on the earth's surface.

4. Which of the following titles best expresses the main idea of the selection?
 - ☐ a. Population Explosion
 - ☐ b. Natural Wonders
 - ☐ c. Use and Abuse
 - ☐ d. Search and Development

5. As opposed to hot spring systems, deep insulated reservoirs
 - ☐ a. must be vented.
 - ☐ b. have less potential.
 - ☐ c. have less pressure.
 - ☐ d. must be drilled.

6. Active volcanoes are not dependable sources of power because their
 - ☐ a. life span is too short.
 - ☐ b. locations are inaccessible.
 - ☐ c. activity is unpredictable.
 - ☐ d. use has never been considered.

7. Hot spring systems are
 - ☐ a. fed from the surface.
 - ☐ b. deep and tightly insulated.
 - ☐ c. rare and difficult to find.
 - ☐ d. relatively inexpensive to develop.

8. The tone of this article is
 - ☐ a. humorous.
 - ☐ b. hysterical.
 - ☐ c. factual.
 - ☐ d. fanciful.

9. In developing geothermal fields for commercial use, geologists appear
 - ☐ a. greedy.
 - ☐ b. creative.
 - ☐ c. reckless.
 - ☐ d. naive.

10. The reference to a group of volcanoes as a "ring of fire" is an example of
 - ☐ a. a simile.
 - ☐ b. a metaphor.
 - ☐ c. an alliteration.
 - ☐ d. an allusion.

Comprehension Skills

1. recalling specific facts	6. making a judgment
2. retaining concepts	7. making an inference
3. organizing facts	8. recognizing tone
4. understanding the main idea	9. understanding characters
5. drawing a conclusion	10. appreciation of literary forms

Study Skills, Part One—Following is a passage with blanks where words have been omitted. Next to the passage are groups of five words, one group for each blank. Complete the passage by selecting the correct word for each of the blanks.

How to Take Notes

It is a disconcerting experience to attend a lecture and discover that you cannot possibly write fast enough to keep up with the speaker. Actually the experience should not be terrifying or frustrating, because a verbatim copy of the lecturer's words is neither ___(1)___ nor necessary.

Notetaking means simply that: taking notes on what the speaker is saying—not making a transcript. To be able to make notes on what is being said, it is important to be listening—not hearing and copying, but listening, and ___(2)___ the presentation.

A common student fault is that of ___(3)___ instead of listening. If you do not understand the lecture in the classroom, you'll never piece it together meaningfully from your notes. The first task of the notetaker, then, is to listen.

The value of notes taken in the classroom lies in their ___(4)___ or recall power. Learn the topic of the lecture and make a note of it. As the speaker progresses, listen to what

(1)
appreciated	useful
requested	accepted	rejected

(2)
understanding	correcting
enjoying	accepting	disliking

(3)
dreaming	sleeping
writing	thinking	laughing

(4)
organization	association
isolation	socialization	development

is being said on the topic and, while listening, jot on paper the gist of the words, enough to trigger later recall of the ___(5)___ .

The way notes are arranged should indicate the organization of the lecture. You should begin with a title for the lecture; this goes at the top of the page. When the speaker changes ___(6)___ start a new page.

Record the notes in an outline style. Main points are listed at the margin, followed by a sentence or two about them. Secondary ideas on the same point should be indented and followed by a sentence of explanation. Further indentions indicate more subordinate ideas. When ___(7)___ the notes, a glance down the left-hand margin will reveal all the main points of the lecture.

(5) situation   listener
     words   ideas   speaker

(6) sources   inflections
     gestures   topics   books

(7) translating   collecting
     rewriting   reviewing   separating

Study Skills, Part Two—Read the study skills passage again, paying special attention to the lesson being taught. Then, without looking back at the passage, complete each sentence below by writing in the missing word or words. Check the Answer Key on page 108 for the answers to Study Skills, Part One, and Study Skills, Part Two.

1. It is impossible to write down all the _____ of the speaker.

2. Your notes should trigger later _____ .

3. The first note should be the _____ of the lecture.

4. Arrangement of your notes should indicate the _____ of the lecture.

5. Notes should be recorded in _____ style.

Answer Key

Selection 1

Vocabulary

1. B	6. B
2. C	7. E
3. E	8. A
4. A	9. D
5. D	10. C

Comprehension

1. b	6. b
2. a	7. b
3. d	8. a
4. c	9. c
5. c	10. d

Study Skills, Part One

1. locating	5. regularly
2. alphabetic-	6. tool
ally	7. complete
3. correctly	
4. fits	

Study Skills, Part Two

1. information
2. page
3. popular
4. appropriate
5. recommended

Selection 2

Vocabulary

1. B	6. D
2. C	7. A
3. E	8. D
4. A	9. E
5. B	10. C

Comprehension

1. b	6. c
2. b	7. d
3. b	8. c
4. c	9. a
5. a	10. a

Study Skills, Part One

1. smooth	6. intended
2. satisfactory	7. thought
3. editing	
4. aloud	
5. errors	

Study Skills, Part Two

1. writing
2. essential
3. sounds
4. confuse
5. ideas

Selection 3

Vocabulary

1. C	6. C
2. B	7. A
3. E	8. E
4. D	9. D
5. B	10. A

Comprehension

1. b	6. c
2. d	7. b
3. b	8. b
4. c	9. b
5. d	10. a

Study Skills, Part One

1. speak	6. technique
2. clear	7. effect
3. number	
4. replace	
5. artificial	

Study Skills, Part Two

1. understand
2. singular
3. feel
4. colorful
5. simple

Selection 4

Vocabulary

1. A	6. A
2. C	7. E
3. D	8. D
4. C	9. E
5. B	10. B

Comprehension

1. d	6. b
2. b	7. a
3. b	8. b
4. a	9. a
5. c	10. c

Study Skills, Part One

1. suitable	6. pictures
2. study	7. become
3. different	
4. models	
5. verbs	

Study Skills, Part Two

1. levels
2. published
3. imitate
4. judged
5. develop

Selection 5

Vocabulary

1. C	6. B
2. A	7. D
3. E	8. E
4. D	9. B
5. C	10. A

Comprehension

1. a	6. a
2. a	7. b
3. d	8. d
4. a	9. b
5. d	10. a

Study Skills, Part One

1. tools	6. long
2. expressing	7. unrelated
3. subject	
4. determining	
5. effectively	

Study Skills, Part Two

1. organization
2. approach
3. views
4. statement
5. limitations

Selection 6

Vocabulary

1. B	6. A
2. C	7. D
3. B	8. C
4. E	9. E
5. D	10. A

Comprehension

1. b	6. c
2. d	7. a
3. b	8. d
4. b	9. c
5. a	10. b

Study Skills, Part One

1. purpose	6. development
2. meaning	7. techniques
3. ineffective	
4. supported	
5. defined	

Study Skills, Part Two

1. select
2. position
3. sense
4. facts
5. acceptable

Selection 7

Vocabulary

1. A	6. B
2. B	7. D
3. D	8. C
4. C	9. E
5. E	10. A

Comprehension

1. a	6. d
2. a	7. c
3. b	8. c
4. c	9. c
5. a	10. a

Study Skills, Part One

1. disorganized 6. transitions
2. confused 7. justified
3. evaluate
4. communication
5. divisions

Study Skills, Part Two

1. subject
2. identify
3. agree
4. logic
5. evidence

Selection 8

Vocabulary

1. A	6. D
2. E	7. B
3. C	8. C
4. A	9. D
5. E	10. B

Comprehension

1. d	6. a
2. a	7. c
3. d	8. a
4. b	9. b
5. c	10. d

Study Skills, Part One

1. words 6. vocabulary
2. how 7. implies
3. context
4. consistent
5. meaning

Study Skills, Part Two

1. incorrect
2. ambiguous
3. effect
4. growth
5. writing

Selection 9

Vocabulary

1. D	6. A
2. C	7. D
3. A	8. B
4. E	9. B
5. C	10. E

Comprehension

1. d	6. a
2. b	7. d
3. a	8. c
4. d	9. c
5. b	10. b

Study Skills, Part One

1. full 6. clues
2. aware 7. guess
3. regularly
4. automatically
5. unknown

Study Skills, Part Two

1. meanings
2. skill
3. common
4. familiarity
5. modify

Selection 10

Vocabulary

1. C	6. D
2. E	7. A
3. D	8. E
4. B	9. B
5. C	10. A

Comprehension

1. c	6. a
2. d	7. a
3. b	8. a
4. d	9. b
5. c	10. c

Study Skills, Part One

1. defined 6. examined
2. assist 7. comparison
3. related
4. expect
5. meaningful

Study Skills, Part Two

1. textbooks
2. items
3. share
4. alike
5. opposite

Selection 11

Vocabulary

1. E	6. A
2. B	7. E
3. A	8. C
4. D	9. B
5. C	10. D

Comprehension

1. c	6. d
2. b	7. d
3. c	8. a
4. d	9. b
5. b	10. d

Study Skills, Part One

1. context 6. mind
2. discover 7. opportunities
3. completing
4. suggest
5. abound

Study Skills, Part Two

1. same
2. mood
3. imagery
4. poetry
5. associations

Selection 12

Vocabulary

1. E	6. C
2. D	7. E
3. A	8. B
4. B	9. C
5. D	10. A

Comprehension

1. d	6. c
2. d	7. d
3. c	8. c
4. b	9. a
5. a	10. b

Study Skills, Part One

1. accompanied 6. effects
2. information 7. encounter
3. recognized
4. always
5. relationship

Study Skills, Part Two

1. adjective
2. apposition
3. further
4. effect
5. intuitively

Selection 13

Vocabulary

1. C	6. E
2. B	7. E
3. A	8. A
4. D	9. D
5. B	10. C

Comprehension

1. d	6. d
2. d	7. b
3. b	8. d
4. c	9. a
5. d	10. b

Study Skills, Part One

1. grades 6. emphasized
2. panic 7. regularly
3. poor
4. reverse
5. preparation

Study Skills, Part Two

1. notes
2. test
3. method
4. class
5. review

Selection 14

Vocabulary
1. A   6. B
2. E   7. B
3. C   8. D
4. A   9. D
5. E   10. C

Comprehension
1. b   6. c
2. b   7. d
3. c   8. a
4. d   9. a
5. b   10. b

Study Skills, Part One
1. confident   6. sufficient
2. task   7. time
3. organized
4. final
5. covered

Study Skills, Part Two
1. save
2. outline
3. spread
4. cramming
5. study

Selection 15

Vocabulary
1. C   6. C
2. D   7. E
3. B   8. A
4. B   9. D
5. A   10. E

Comprehension
1. a   6. c
2. a   7. d
3. a   8. b
4. d   9. b
5. a   10. c

Study Skills, Part One
1. fresh   6. generalizations
2. instructor   7. selective
3. contestant
4. brief
5. study

Study Skills, Part Two
1. approach
2. imagination
3. outline
4. main
5. elements

Selection 16

Vocabulary
1. B   6. A
2. A   7. C
3. D   8. E
4. E   9. B
5. D   10. C

Comprehension
1. b   6. b
2. a   7. d
3. b   8. b
4. d   9. b
5. c   10. d

Study Skills, Part One
1. beforehand   6. suitable
2. Essay   7. legitimately
3. label
4. alert
5. taken

Study Skills, Part Two
1. exam
2. objective
3. instructors
4. course
5. information

Selection 17

Vocabulary
1. A   6. C
2. B   7. B
3. D   8. A
4. D   9. C
5. E   10. E

Comprehension
1. c   6. d
2. b   7. d
3. b   8. c
4. d   9. b
5. a   10. b

Study Skills, Part One
1. tests   6. major
2. repeat   7. preparation
3. again
4. significant
5. intensive

Study Skills, Part Two
1. questions
2. class
3. review
4. cramming
5. performances

Selection 18

Vocabulary
1. E   6. D
2. C   7. A
3. B   8. E
4. A   9. C
5. B   10. D

Comprehension
1. c   6. a
2. c   7. b
3. d   8. b
4. b   9. a
5. d   10. b

Study Skills, Part One
1. similar   6. think
2. follow   7. difficult
3. wrong
4. advantage
5. immediately

Study Skills, Part Two
1. multiple choice
2. all
3. time
4. three
5. last

Selection 19

Vocabulary
1. D   6. B
2. B   7. C
3. D   8. E
4. A   9. C
5. E   10. A

Comprehension
1. a   6. b
2. d   7. c
3. d   8. a
4. c   9. a
5. a   10. d

Study Skills, Part One
1. use   6. lacking
2. compose   7. handwriting
3. Confine
4. subject
5. credit

Study Skills, Part Two
1. written
2. forgotten
3. transferred
4. short
5. readable

Selection 20

Vocabulary
1. E   6. E
2. A   7. D
3. C   8. C
4. D   9. B
5. B   10. A

Comprehension
1. a   6. c
2. b   7. a
3. c   8. c
4. d   9. b
5. d   10. b

Study Skills, Part One
1. useful   6. topics
2. understanding   7. reviewing
3. writing
4. association
5. ideas

Study Skills, Part Two
1. words
2. recall
3. topic
4. organization
5. outline

Bibliography

Every effort has been made to locate the author, publisher, place of publication, and copyright date for each selection.

Benkovitch, Robert. "The Plight of the Porpoise." In *National Humane Review.* Denver: American Humane Association, 1973.

Ferderber, Skip. "The Duck Man of Venice." In *National Humane Review.* Denver: American Humane Association, 1972.

Gentry, Bern. "Sickle-Cell Anemia." In *Future* magazine. United States Jaycees.

Gonzalez, Arturo. "Atlantis: Legend Lives On." In *Aramco World.* Arabian Oil Company.

Halegood, Rog. "The Anatomy of Drink." In *Future* magazine. United States Jaycees.

——— . "The Selling of the Flesh." In *Future* magazine. United States Jaycees.

Lionel, Robert. "Dying, One Day at a Time." In *Future* magazine. United States Jaycees.

Nolan, M.D., William A. "Mononucleosis: The Overtreated Disease." In *McCall's* magazine. New York: McCall Publishing Company, 1974.

Reiss, Jr., Albert J. "Police Brutality: Answers to Key Questions." In *Transaction.* Transaction, Inc., 1968.

Richards, Norman. "Are You Really Ready For the Highways?" In *Marathon World.* Marathon Oil Company.

Saki [H. H. Munro]. "The Interlopers." In *The Complete Short Stories of Saki.* New York: The Viking Press.

Salomon, Dr. Milton. "Organic Gardening in Perspective."

Trecker, Janice Law. "Textbooks and the Invisible Woman." Council on Interracial Books for Children.

Wolff, Anthony. "Dr. Batman." In *Saturday Review/World.* New York: Saturday Review, 1974.

——— . "New Use for Old Cars."

"Natural Steam for Power."

"The Right to Exist."

Words per Minute

Selection / No. of Words	1	2	3	4	5	6	7	8	9	10	11	12	13	14	15	16	17	18	19	20
No. of Words	1585	1230	1460	1610	1520	1775	1360	1290	1650	1590	1845	1800	2200	2160	1560	1510	1310	1620	1420	1440
1:20	1220	925	1100	1210	1145	1335	1025	970	1240	1195	1385	1355	1655	1625	1175	1135	985	1220	1070	1085
1:40	990	740	880	970	915	1070	820	775	995	960	1110	1085	1325	1300	940	910	790	975	855	865
2:00	790	615	730	805	760	890	680	645	825	795	925	900	1100	1080	780	755	655	810	710	720
2:20	690	530	625	690	650	760	585	555	710	680	790	775	945	925	670	650	560	695	610	620
2:40	610	460	550	605	570	665	510	485	620	600	695	675	825	810	585	570	490	610	535	540
3:00	560	410	485	535	505	590	455	430	550	530	615	600	735	720	520	505	435	540	475	480
3:20	510	370	440	485	455	535	410	385	495	475	555	540	660	650	470	455	395	485	425	430
3:40	440	335	400	440	415	485	370	350	450	435	505	490	600	590	425	415	360	445	395	395
4:00	395	310	365	405	380	445	340	325	415	400	460	450	550	540	390	380	330	405	355	360
4:20	370	285	335	370	350	410	315	300	380	365	425	415	510	500	360	350	305	375	330	335
4:40	345	265	315	345	325	380	290	275	355	340	395	385	470	465	335	325	280	350	305	310
5:00	315	245	290	320	305	355	270	260	330	320	370	360	440	430	310	300	260	325	285	290
5:20	300	230	275	300	285	335	255	240	310	300	345	340	415	405	295	285	245	305	265	270
5:40	285	215	260	285	270	315	240	230	290	280	325	320	390	380	275	265	230	285	250	255
6:00	265	205	245	270	255	295	225	215	275	265	310	300	365	360	260	250	220	270	235	240
6:20	250	195	230	255	240	280	215	205	260	250	290	285	350	340	245	240	205	255	225	230
6:40	240	185	220	240	230	265	205	195	250	240	275	270	330	325	235	225	195	245	215	215
7:00	225	175	210	230	215	255	195	185	235	225	265	255	315	310	225	215	185	230	205	205
7:20	215	170	200	220	205	240	185	175	225	215	250	245	300	295	215	205	180	220	195	195
7:40	210	160	190	210	200	230	180	170	215	210	240	235	285	280	205	195	170	210	185	190
8:00	200	155	185	200	190	220	170	160	205	200	230	225	275	270	195	190	165	205	180	180
8:20	190	150	175	195	180	215	165	155	200	190	220	215	265	260	185	180	155	195	170	175
8:40	185	140	170	185	175	205	155	150	190	185	215	210	255	250	180	175	150	185	165	165
9:00	175	135	160	180	170	195	150	145	185	175	205	200	245	240	175	170	145	180	160	160
9:20	170	130	155	175	165	190	145	140	175	170	200	195	235	230	165	160	140	175	150	155
9:40	165	125	150	165	160	185	140	135	170	165	190	185	230	225	160	155	135	170	145	150
10:00	160	125	145	160	150	180	135	130	165	160	185	180	220	215	155	150	130	160	140	145
10:20	155	120	140	155	145	170	130	125	160	155	180	175	215	210	150	145	125	155	135	140
10:40	150	115	135	150	145	165	130	120	155	150	175	170	205	205	145	140	125	150	135	135
11:00	145	110	135	145	140	160	125	120	150	145	170	165	200	195	140	135	120	145	130	130
11:20	140	110	130	140	135	155	120	115	145	140	165	160	195	190	140	135	115	145	125	130
11:40	135	105	125	140	130	150	115	110	140	135	160	155	190	185	135	130	110	140	120	125
12:00	130	105	120	135	125	150	115	110	135	135	155	150	185	180	130	125	110	135	120	120
12:20	130	100	120	130	125	145	110	105	130	130	150	145	180	175	125	120	105	130	115	115
12:40	125	95	115	125	120	140	105	100	125	125	145	140	175	170	125	120	105	130	110	115
13:00	120	95	110	125	115	135	105	100	125	120	140	140	170	165	120	115	100	125	110	110
13:20	120	90	110	120	115	135	100	95	120	120	140	135	165	160	115	110	100	120	105	110
13:40	115	90	105	120	110	130	100	95	120	115	135	130	160	160	110	110	95	120	105	105
14:00	115	90	105	115	110	125	95	90	115	115	130	130	155	155	110	105	95	115	100	105
14:20	110	85	100	110	105	125	95	90	115	110	130	125	155	150	105	105	90	115	100	100
14:40	110	85	100	110	105	120	95	90	110	110	125	125	150	145	105	105	90	110	95	100
15:00	105	80	95	105	100	120	90	85	110	105	125	120	145	145	105	100	85	110	95	85

Minutes and Seconds Elapsed

Progress Graph

		Scores															
Selection	Words per Minute	100	90	80	70	60	50	40	30	20							
1																	
2																	
3																	
4																	
5																	
6																	
7																	
8																	
9																	
10																	
11																	
12																	
13																	
14																	
15																	
16																	
17																	
18																	
19																	
20																	

Comprehension Skills Profile

The graph below is designed to help you see your areas of comprehension weakness. Because all the comprehension questions in this text are coded, it is possible for you to determine which kinds of questions give you the most trouble.

On the graph below, keep a record of questions you have answered incorrectly. Following each selection, darken a square on the graph next to the number of the question missed. The columns are labeled with the selection numbers.

By looking at the chart and noting the number of shaded squares, you should be able to tell which areas of comprehension you are weak in. A large number of shaded squares across from a particular skill signifies an area of reading comprehension weakness. When you discover a particular weakness, give greater attention and time to answering questions of that type.

Further, you might wish to check with your instructor for recommendations of appropriate practice materials.

Selection

Categories of Comprehension Skills	1	2	3	4	5	6	7	8	9	10	11	12	13	14	15	16	17	18	19	20
1. Recalling Specific Facts																				
2. Retaining Concepts																				
3. Organizing Facts																				
4. Understanding the Main Idea																				
5. Drawing a Conclusion																				
6. Making a Judgment																				
7. Making an Inference																				
8. Recognizing Tone																				
9. Understanding Characters																				
10. Appreciation of Literary Forms																				